HENRY VIII AND LUTHER

HENRY VIII AND LUTHER

AN ACCOUNT OF
THEIR PERSONAL RELATIONS

BY
ERWIN DOERNBERG

WITH A FOREWORD BY
THE REV. PROF. G. E. RUPP

STANFORD UNIVERSITY PRESS
STANFORD CALIFORNIA

© 1961 by Erwin Doernberg
All rights reserved
Printed in Great Britain

942.052
D674

143437

DA
332
.D6
1961

TO MY WIFE

CONTENTS

LIST OF ILLUSTRATIONS

Plates I and II

Henry VIII's book *Assertio Septem Sacramentorum,* first edition (1521). Title page and (overleaf) advertisement of the Papal Indulgence granted to the reader
facing pages 16 and 17

Plate III

Luther's reply to Henry VIII's book, Latin Version, (1522). Title page
facing page 32

Plate IV

Thomas Murner's Tract *Whether the King of England or Luther is a Liar* (1523). Title page
facing page 64

Plates V and VI

The King's reply to Luther's offer of an apology of 1525 (1526). The end of Luther's letter and (overleaf) the opening of Henry VIII's answer
facing pages 80 and 81

All are reproduced by courtesy of the Trustees of the British Museum

FOREWORD

The main lines of the story of the English Reformation under Henry VIII have been so often described that it is often assumed that there is no new material, no new assessment necessary. This is far from being true, and especially in the details of the relation between what happened in this island, and the happenings on the Continent, too much has been left to those who have exaggerated or played down the importance of these cross-currents for dogmatic reasons. In this book Erwin Doernberg has performed a most useful service by putting together in one volume the diverse strands which relate Henry VIII to the Lutheran Reformers: the fiery debate between Henry and Martin Luther: the intricate issues involved in Henry's divorce, the intermittent angling of Henry with the Protestant princes of the Schmalkaldic league. Mr. Doernberg makes available the findings of a number of German works hitherto hardly used in this country. He has gone to the English sources and blended old and new material in a readable and balanced narrative. Many readers will be interested to read what Henry and Luther had to say about one another in a fuller account than has hitherto been given in English secondary sources. The book is therefore greatly to be welcomed, and I am sure that teachers and students will turn to it for some time to come, while the story itself has its own interest for the general reader.

GORDON RUPP

University of Manchester
October 1960

xi

PREFACE

As it is not possible to write on the English Reformation with olympian indifference, any book on any of its aspects must inevitably displease some of its readers. It will become obvious to my readers that I have little liking for Henry VIII and even less for this King's reformation of the Church. Yet I hope to have succeeded in my aim to accord him fair treatment. Throughout it has been my intention not to produce yet another book on the Reformation with evidence selected, suppressed or arranged to fit the writer's bias. With the maximum of objectivity given to me, I have described a series of historical events.

Luther stands out in these pages as the one truly religious and upright personality. No reader need be made uncomfortable by this fact; in the company of Henry VIII, Leo X and Clement VII it could hardly be otherwise. The first half of the sixteenth century was not the most illustrious period of either the papacy or of the Church of England; if this, the finest period of the Lutheran Church, were to be compared with more respectable epochs of the Roman Catholic and Anglican Churches, the result might possibly be less favourable to Luther. Be that as it may, such wider comparison does not concern us here, as we are dealing only with the years from 1521 to approximately 1540.

It is advisable to read this book as a whole, not as a sequence of richly contrasting episodes. In a bewildering chain of fickle, ever-shifting changes, one factor remains constant: Henry VIII is always in control. I know that one can simplify matters by proposing that Henry was good before 1529 and bad ever after, or vice versa. My own impression is, it was the same Henry throughout.

The bibliography indicates that I have made ample and

grateful use of the works of many historians who have written on the period of Henry VIII. It includes, of course, works by authors whose point of view I cannot share, but whose bias I find as forgivable as I hope mine may be held to be. It even includes some books which contain misleading opinions written, I must suspect, quite deliberately; to avoid making my book unnecessarily controversial I have suppressed the urge to display examples. Of course, I have drawn the line when I felt that a writer had forfeited my respect altogether. Absence of reference to, say, J. Maritain's *Three Reformers* should not therefore lead anybody to believe that I had not read it.

Quotations from documents in contemporary English are reproduced in the spelling of the indicated secondary sources; some of the editors have modernized the texts more or less drastically. Passages translated from Latin or German originals appear, of course, in modern English and lack therefore the linguistic charm of the old English quotations. Such inconsistency is most regrettable but could not be avoided.

From time to time I had to summarize quite briefly the general historical background of my narrowly defined subject. Such sketches are invariably rather inadequate and are only introduced to provide the necessary general context. I trust that this book contains sufficient material which is unknown, and yet highly interesting, to warrant the briefest possible treatment of the general events, which have been so often described.

Miss Jane Wilson has been a helpfully critical reader of my manuscript and I am most grateful to the Trustees of the British Museum for the permission to publish reproductions from four books.

Southgate, November 1960   E.D.

HENRY VIII AND LUTHER

Part I

HENRY VIII's BOOK AGAINST LUTHER AND LUTHER'S REPLY

1

NOBODY can tell with any certainty what was Henry VIII's motive in writing a refutation of Luther's book *De Captivitate Babylonica Ecclesiae*. There are three possibilities: firstly, Henry VIII may have been genuinely affected by Luther's reformative activities; secondly, he may have been aware of the significance of Luther as a formidable embarrassment to the papacy and seen this as an excellent opportunity to obtain a long-desired papal title from Leo X; or there may have been a mixture of motives partly originating from a sincere concern for the threatened religious traditions, partly from a calculation of the political effect if, at such a time, he were to voice in uncompromising terms his support of the Pope.

Henry VIII showed a dislike of Lutheran teaching throughout his life. After 1531 this may have been influenced, at least in part, by the fact that Luther calmly but with adamant firmness refused to declare his approval of Henry's separation from Queen Catherine, however hard the King tried to gain a favourable verdict from Wittenberg. The fact that Lutheran sympathies troubled Henry only on brief and often almost irrelevant occasions, seems due to Luther's rather than to Henry's constancy in theological matters. Henry VIII remained favourably disposed to causes or persons only as long as they could be expected to be useful for his own schemes. Therefore, even if Luther had obliged the King with an approval of the divorce, nobody can surmise what Henry's reaction would have been in the long run; the Supreme Head of the Church of England might have turned Lutheran for a few weeks, a few months or years, perhaps permanently, or perhaps not at all. Henry was too unpredictable to be the object of such conjecture; it is difficult enough to follow him through the maze of changes which actually took place, almost as difficult for the historian in the twentieth century as it was for his contemporaries.

Henry VIII's motives have frequently been so dubious that they easily lend themselves to interpretations inspired by the interpreter's own more permanent persuasions. Catholic writers, therefore, tend to be absolutely certain of the King's disinterested zeal for the papacy at the time when he wrote against Luther, whilst Protestant writers have a tendency to see in Henry's book against Luther an instance of the King's undoubted genius for making swift use of the plight of another in the promotion of his personal devices. *De facto* we do not know what prompted Henry to write against Luther. Contemporary opinion does not help us either. Those in his immediate surroundings testify invariably to the most noble of intentions in Henry's actions, but the flattery of courtiers is not evidence. It is useless to announce one's own answer to the question. The best thing to do in the circumstances is to content oneself with a narrative of the events.

2

On January 28th, 1521, the Diet of Worms was officially opened and throughout the month there had been discussions about Luther, particularly whether it would be legitimate to allow him to appear in person, considering that he stood already under the papal interdict. Henry's ambassador to Charles V was Cuthbert Tunstall, at the time Master of the Rolls, Vice-Chancellor and Archdeacon of Chester. On January 29th Tunstall wrote to Wolsey mentioning Luther's book, published in 1520, *De Captivitate Babylonica Ecclesiae*: '... wherin he upholdith that iiij off the sacraments be allonly de iure posituo, viz: confirmatio, ordo, extrema vnctio, et matrimonium, which alonly by the popis ordinaunce be callyd sacraments, and that baptising, eucharistia, et penitentia be de iure diunis et evangelio, which boke is intitylde De Babylonica Captiutate Ecclesiae. They say ther is moch moo strange opinions in hit nere to the opinions off boheme. I pray god kep that boke out off englond. . . .'[1] Tunstall left Worms just before Luther's arrival and we are therefore left without a report which, no doubt, would have been full of great interest.

On April 16th, 1521—the day of Luther's arrival in Worms —Secretary Pace wrote to Cardinal Wolsey that he had found the King reading a new book of Luther's. This was, indeed, the *Babylonian Captivity of the Church*. The King had 'dispraised' the book and Pace had shown him a copy of the papal bull against the reformer. The secretary's report continues: 'at which the king was well contented, showing unto me that it was joyous to have those tidings from the pope's holiness at such time, as he had taken upon him the defence of Christ's Church with his pen afore the receipt of such tidings; and that he will make an end of his book within these (few days); and desiring your grace to provide that within the same space all such as be appointed to examine Luther's writings may be congregated for his highness' perceiving.'

Pace further informed Wolsey of the King's intention that the book he was writing was to be sent 'not only to Rome, but also into France and other nations as shall appear convenient. So that all the Church is more bound to this good and virtuous prince for the vehement zeal he beareth unto the same than I can express'.[2]

For an assessment of the King's true motive there seems to be some significance in the anticipation and precise definition of the approval he expected, particularly in the hint that he wished it to be understood that he had come to *defend the Church*.

Already in 1517 Henry VIII had been at work on a theological treatise which, at Cardinal Wolsey's suggestion, was to be turned into a refutation of Luther's *Ninety-Five Theses against Indulgences* which Luther had published on October 31st that year and which had probably reached England very soon afterwards. Considering how quickly these *Theses* had become known throughout Germany and her neighbouring countries, it seems unlikely that they were a novelty in England when, on March 5th, 1518, Erasmus sent a copy accompanied by a letter to Sir Thomas More. We know that since 1515 Henry VIII had been anxious to obtain a papal title, by his own preference *Defensor Ecclesiae* or *Fidei*, and it seems likely that already the theological task of 1517 was set in pursuance of this aim. However, hardly anything is known about the earlier work of the King and it appears that it remained unfinished. It is generally assumed that Henry made use of these sketches when writing the *Assertion of the Seven Sacraments* of 1521. In any event, the introductory chapter of the book, bearing the title *Of Indulgences and of the Pope's Authority*, seems to be far better adapted to the controversies of 1517–18 than to the contents of the *Babylonian Captivity*. What Henry wrote about indulgences hardly makes any approach to the essential theological points of the subject, points which had become widely known through the disputations which had followed Luther's action of 1517. By 1521, when the *Assertion of the Seven Sacraments* was written, the controversy about indulgences had come to an end as far as Luther was concerned, and so shallow a treatment at so late a time could not possibly have had any influence on anything or anyone. Luther's *Babylonian Captivity* contains only a very short note on the subject of indulgences, in which Luther reminded his readers that his earlier writings on the matter (in which he had only aimed at the correction of stark abuse) were no longer valid. He offered his thanks to his opponents for having troubled him with their attention and for having made him work hard; consequently he had learned so much about indulgences that he had now arrived at recommending their total dismissal. The passage in which he made this announcement is so lightly written that it cannot be made the basis for a disputation. Henry's elaborate introduction to the *Assertio Septem Sacramentorum* could not possibly have been provoked by those few sentences of Luther's on a subject which in fact already belonged to history. What Henry wrote may then have derived from an earlier time. His previous sketch is not explicitly mentioned in the book, but he may have referred to it in his letter to the Pope of May 21st, 1521, when mentioning that 'ever since he knew of Luther's heresy in Germany, he had made it his study how to extirpate it'.[3]

3

Lutheran writings reached England between 1517 and 1529 in considerable quantities and the imports continued despite all attempts to suppress them. It seems that for a time they were not taken too seriously. From 1520 onwards, letters from Rome to Cardinal Wolsey on the subject of Lutheran books became ever more insistent. Wolsey had, of course, been inclined against Lutheran influences from the outset, but one could hardly expect a prelate so preoccupied with state affairs to arrive quickly at an appreciation of Luther's true significance, save perhaps as a threat to the kind of established order which he represented almost to excess as multiple pluralist (Archbishop of York; Bishop of Durham and Winchester; deputizing, 'farming' for non-resident alien bishops, at Worcester, Salisbury and Llandaff; and lastly even Abbot of St. Albans); and this is but the most spectacular aspect of his ecclesiastical power.* There was a time when he corresponded with Erasmus on the subject of Luther's activities, but this was in 1519 when Erasmus kept all the world guessing as to whether he was a mild supporter or a mild critic of the reformer.

On May 18th, 1519, Erasmus wrote to Wolsey one of his typical, carefully expressed letters of the period in which he cautiously balanced praise for Luther's character and broader aims against even more cautious statements that he had not read any of his writings ('His conduct is so blameless that even his opponents cannot find anything with which to reproach him'). Wolsey, Sir Thomas More, Bishop Cuthbert Tunstall and many others tried again and again to enlist Erasmus's assistance in their struggle against Lutheran influences. However, for many years he continued to maintain that he had not read the reformer's books, that only rumours of their content had reached him, that he was neither unsympathetic towards Luther's original intentions, nor critical of his zeal, that he was not at all supporting him, that he was not in a position to write against him, and so forth.[4] On one occasion, in 1523, he went as far as writing to Tunstall that he considered some moderation advisable 'lest we not merely pluck up the wheat with the tares, but actually pluck up wheat instead of tares'. Charles V, Duke George of Saxony, the Popes Leo X, Adrian VI and Clement VII all pressed him

*Wolsey's illegitimate son was, as a youth, Dean of Wells, Archdeacon of York and Richmond, had two rectories, six prebends and one appointment as chancellor.

to write against Luther. By 1523 a situation had arisen in
which Erasmus could no longer maintain neutrality and he
chose to write against Luther's conception of the determin-
ism of the will. He sent a preliminary draft to Henry VIII and
wrote letters to Wolsey, Archbishop Warham, Bishop Fisher
and Bishop Tunstall, announcing his book *De Libero Arbitrio*.
However pleased Henry VIII was with the book, the correspondence soon reverted to the former insistent wishes that
Erasmus would continue writing more anti-Lutheran books.
As late as September 1527, Henry VIII still thought Erasmus
could be induced to come to England and to write against
Luther under his protection.[5] The King and the humanist had
once before discussed Luther, on the occasion of a meeting in
1520. Unfortunately the report of Frederick Myconius on
that meeting does not reveal to us whether the conversation
had any influence on Henry's future intentions. In any case,
the correspondence between Wolsey and Erasmus had no
repercussions at all.

It was not until 1521 that Wolsey was really urgently requested to take severe action. Already Tunstall had written to
him from Worms with the request 'that yor grace may cal
befor you the printers and bokesellers and gyff them a strayte
charge that they bring noon off his bokes into englond, nor
that they translate noon off them into english, lest theby
myght ensue grete troble to the realme and church off englond, as is now her'.[6] Soon afterwards, a letter reached
Wolsey from Rome, written by the Cardinal de Medici and
containing a gentle yet distinct rebuke: 'The pope commends
Wolsey's design', the summary reads, 'of not suffering those
books to be imported or sold, but thinks that remedy would
not be sufficient, as so many have already got abroad and
they can be circulated by other means than the booksellers.
A general bonfire would be more satisfactory.'[7] Archbishop
Warham, too, expressed acute anxiety about the threat of
Lutheran influences in England, having been informed by
the Bishop of Lincoln about the popularity of the Lutheran
books in Oxford. He wrote to the Cardinal:

'Please it your Grace to understand that now lately I re-
ceyvid letters from the Universitie of Oxford, and in those
same certayne newes whiche I am very sorry to here. For I am

enformyd that diverse of that Universitie be infectyd with the heresyes of Luther and of others of that sorte, havyng emong theym a grete nombre of books of the saide perverse doctrine which wer forboden by your Graces auctoritie as Legate de latere of the See apostolique, and also by me as Chauncellor of the saide Universitie, to be hadd, kept, or redd by any person off the same, except suche as wer licensed to have thayme to impugne and convince the erroneus opinions conteyned in theym. But it is a sorrowful thing to see how gredyly inconstaunt men, and specyally inexpert youthe, fallith to newe doctrynes be they never so pestilent; and howe prone they be to attempt that thing that they be forbeden of thair superiors for thair ouyne welthe. . . .

'Pytie yt were that through the lewdnes of on or two cankerd members, whiche as I understand have enducyd no small nombre of yong and incircumspect foles to geve ere unto thaym, the hole Universitie shuld run in thinfamy of soo haynouse a cryme, the heryng wherof shuld be right delectable and plesant to the open Lutheranes beyond the See, and secrete behyther, wherof they wold take hart and confydence that theyr pestilent doctrynes shuld encrese and multiply, seying bothe the Universities of Inglande enfectid therwith, wherof the on hathe many yeeres been voyd of all heresyes, and the other hather afore nowe take apon hyr the prayse that she was never defylyd; and nevertheles nowe she is thought to be the originall occasion and cause of the fall of Oxford.

'By thes my writing I entende in nowise to move, but that the capytaynes of the said erroneus doctrynes be punishede to the ferefull example of all other. But if all the hole nombyr of yong scolers suspectyd in this cause (which as the Universitie writieth to me be marvelouse sory and repentaunt that ever they had any such boks, or redde or herde any of Luther's opynyons) shuld be callyd up to London, yt shuld engendre grete obloquy and sclandre to the Universitie, bothe behyther the See and beyonde, to the sorrow of all good men, and the pleasure of heretyks, desyring to have many folowers of thayr mischef; and (as it is thought) the less brute the better, ffor thavoyding wherof the said Universitie hath desyred me to move your Grace to be so good and gracyouse unto thaym, to gyve in commission to some sadd father which was brought up in the said Universitie of Oxford to syt ther, and examyne, not the hedds (which it may please your Grace to reserve to your own examination) but the novicyes which be not yet throughly cankerd in the said errors. . . .'

Then he advised Wolsey that in his opinion not only Luther's books should be forbidden but also those of his adherents, 'for I understand ther be many of thos newe writers as yll as Luther. And therfor it needeth this gret provision to be made for stopping of thaym, as of Luthers. . . .'[8]

That Warham recommended the Heads to Wolsey's personal admonition had its special, somewhat delicate reason: these 'capytaines' of Lutheranism in Oxford happened to be the scholars whom Wolsey himself had transferred from Cambridge for the staffing of his own foundation, 'Cardinal College'.

The solemn burning of Lutheran books in London took place on May 12th, 1521, following Wolsey's proclamation that all writings of Luther had to be delivered to the bishop or his deputy. An appendix to the proclamation listed forty-two doctrines, some of them quite wild and fantastic, presumed to be Lutheran. The aim of the bonfire was to stamp out 'those damnable and pestiferous errors and heresies broached by Luther . . . in this kingdom, lest they should take root as a noxious briar here; and that by the express will and command of the most potent and illustrious prince . . . [who had ordered Wolsey] with all possible endeavour to root out and abolish this heresy from this noble kingdom.'[9]

Wolsey presided in the presence of the papal nuncio, the Archbishop of Canterbury, the imperial ambassador and the Bishop of London. John Fisher, Bishop of Rochester, preached a long sermon. Wolsey, however, acted with remarkable restraint, imposing only mild penances on those people who were found to be contaminated.[10] Bishop Fisher's sermon was printed in Latin and also in a translation by Richard Pace. Later, these books became very uncomfortable for Henry VIII who issued repeated proclamations ordering all copies to be sent to Cromwell for destruction.

The success of the fire was only temporary; most certainly not all the books had been handed over and very soon new importations and new printing activities took place.

Various estimates have been made as to the extent of the Lutheran influence in England. It is certainly not the case that 'the flame raised by Luther in Germany was quite unintelligible to Englishmen at large'.[11] The contemporary authorities were clearly of a different opinion as we realize from their resolute attempts to combat the influence by all possible means. Neither does it seem quite right to presume, as is so frequently done, that the Lutheran influence was practically restricted to isolated cliques such as the group of men who used to meet regularly at the White Horse Inn at Cambridge. Cuthbert Tunstall, as Bishop of London, was deeply concerned with the widespread popularity of Lutheran books in his diocese and Sir Thomas More, too, had reason to take action in the capital. In 1526 he arranged for an elaborate visitation of the German merchants of the Hanse, in Steelyard, without informing them in advance of his object and, therefore, alarming them considerably. A printed newsletter from the alderman addressed to the burgomaster and the town council of Cologne reports that 'Herr Thomas Moir' quickly assured the nervous merchants that there was no special reason for them to be apprehensive. After making the announcement that one of their number had been put into prison for clipping coins, he at last came to the main point of the spectacular show, the stern prohibition against further importations of Lutheran literature.[12] Indeed, there cannot be any doubt that the Hanse merchants had been active in the traffic of books. In February 1526 four of them were found guilty of propagating Lutheran writings when tried, together with Robert Barnes, by the Bishops of London, Rochester and Bath and St. Asaph's. Barnes was on trial for his heretical Cambridge sermon of December 24th, 1525. All five were condemned to carry faggots at St. Paul's.

Two years later, on March 7th, 1528, Bishop Tunstall gave a special dispensation to Sir Thomas More permitting him to read the prohibited books in order to refute Luther in the vernacular.[13] The suppression of books was not only troublesome but costly, and Archbishop Warham had to ask his suffragans for contributions towards the purchase of Lutheran books for burning.[14] All these men who were so acutely conscious of their responsibility to keep Lutheran influences at bay were busy persons who would hardly have devoted so much of their energy and time to the task had they not regarded it as highly important.

The booksellers, of course, gave the authorities endless trouble. On October 12th, 1524, some of them were reprimanded by Bishop Tunstall who warned them not to import into England books printed in Germany, or any other books containing Lutheran heresies, nor to sell such books. No current foreign books must be sold before being shown for approval to Cardinal Wolsey, the Bishop of London or the Bishop of Rochester.[15] Two years later, on October 25th, 1526, a much larger assembly of booksellers had to appear before the Bishop and the admonitions were repeated. More comprehensive safeguards were introduced: all printing in the country, both of English and of foreign books, was now to be controlled by a system of ecclesiastical licence.[16] Yet a Royal Proclamation of 1530 demonstrates that all this was of no avail and that the importation and sales of Lutheran books continued; the proclamation repeats the prohibition: such works must not be imported, sold, accepted or kept, irrespective as to whether they were printed or in manuscript.[17]

During the same years, lists of forbidden books were compiled. The first 'index' of 1526[18] listed eighteen books, including some works of Luther and one each of Huss, Zwingli and Bentz; the second index of 1529 contained eighty-five titles, including twenty-two by Luther.[19] It is interesting to note that by 1529 fines were no longer to be paid to the Church, but to Henry VIII's own exchequer. The Church authorities had to provide for the expenses of the secular officers engaged in apprehending offenders. The sheriffs were instructed to turn over all persons charged with violation of the proclamation to the ecclesiastical courts for trial, but upon conviction they had to be returned for punishment to the secular authorities.[20]

It has been suggested[21] that Henry VIII's index of forbidden books of 1526 was the first of its kind. While it is indeed true that the first papal index was published only in 1559, lists of the kind had been compiled in Belgium under Charles V since 1524 and particularly in 1526.[22] In the compilation of the later continental indexes no use was made of the English lists; a glance at the Henrican indexes shows that they were

obviously compiled in conjunction with recent book importations and therefore listed a chance collection of titles.

All this leaves us in no doubt that there was a strong interest in Lutheran literature in England. Yet one cannot possibly
say there was anything in the nature of a religious crisis in the
country which would have caused English people to react
to these writings with the intensity that large sections of the
Germans had done. There was in England, as in all other
countries, a strong resentment against the popes, against the
clergy, against certain abuses; such critical resentment was
by no means confined to those countries which eventually
separated themselves from obedience to Rome and it was
current, in one form or another, throughout the Middle Ages.
The sermons and lectures of Dean Colet (d. 1519) are well
suited to characterize the kind of reform envisaged time and
time again by moralists. Sharp criticism of the Church temporal and a call for 'reform in head and members' (a medieval
slogan) could and did go well with fundamental conformity
and has, as such, nothing to do with heresy in general nor
with Lutheranism in particular. Thus, although there was
undoubtedly a certain amount of dissatisfaction in England
in 1521, when Henry VIII resolved to write against Luther,
this need by no means be interpreted as a budding reformation akin to the Lutheran pattern. The English complaint
was more concerned with the power of the papal legates than
with the popes, more with fiscal matters and questions of
morals, jurisdiction and power in Church government than
with theological, doctrinal problems. To be sure, the Lutheran reformation had also begun with an acute, local problem
—Tetzel's sale of an indulgence for the Archbishop of Mainz
—but, owing to Luther, it concerned itself right from the beginning with doctrine rather than confining itself to the mere
correction of a particular abuse. The astonishing reaction
throughout Germany and some of her neighbouring countries
revealed (and nobody was more astonished than Luther himself) that a deeply felt religious crisis had reached its climax.

The character of what there was of a more specifically
religious unrest in England is well illustrated in a recent book
by Professor A. G. Dickens, *Lollards and Protestants in the
Diocese of York, 1509–1558.* Some verbatim reports of actual
conversations of a heretical nature demonstrate that remnants

of Lollard sentiments were still current among some sections
of the people; but they also show that most of those latter-
day Lollards were marvellously confused about the specific
things which, they thought, annoyed them. It is interesting to
know what excited ignorant and opinionated grumblers like
James Hardcastell, a butcher of Barwick-in-Elmet; and how
the fourth Earl of Shrewsbury, a great beneficiary of Henry
VIII, argued with a heretic. However, these doings have
their own level and are not by any means identical with
Lutheran theology. Discontent in England, in all its mani-
festations, was not amounting to a religious crisis. Of the
English Reformation it is much truer to say it *created* a
religious crisis and uncertainties, some of which continue to
this day.

4

Notwithstanding her jealousy of foreign interference and
power, her resentment of alien papal legates and financial
extortion, there is no doubt that England, as a nation, was
not a problem for the papacy at the time when Henry VIII
issued his book against Luther, however much satisfaction
an apparently increasing number of people derived from
reading heretical literature.

Of course, when we consider what happened in the world
during those years, the political constellations of the time
have to be examined no less than the purely religious aspects.
Not only secular potentates but ecclesiastics of all grades were
no doubt preoccupied with political affairs to a much larger
extent than with pastoral matters. Cardinal Wolsey was, as
a type, certainly representative of powerful prelates of the
period. Is it not significant that this superb statesman's writings include nothing at all of a theological nature?[23] Had it
been otherwise, the Church, and particularly Rome, would
most certainly have reacted much more strongly to the first
stages of Luther's activities of 1517–18. When it was too late
it became desirable—a desperate substitute for effective
counter-arguments—to seize on Luther's person. Even after
seven years, in 1524, certain highly placed prelates had not
yet grasped that Luther's mentality was quite different from

their own; they thought the worst was over when a rumour reached them that the Pope was considering making Luther a cardinal in order to silence him.[24] A cardinal's hat had, indeed, been offered to Erasmus; in this case it was, of course, not the intention to silence a man, but to induce him to write against Luther (or, at least, to gain certainty about his loyalty to the Catholic cause).

If the Pope and important prelates were almost fully occupied with political activity and personal ambitions, the same was surely the case with a secular ruler such as the King of England.

It is impossible to summarize in a few sentences the amazing, ever-shifting scene in which Charles V, Francis I and the Pope endeavoured to advance their conflicting interests, with Cardinal Wolsey in the background as mediator, universal judge, peacemaker, peace preventer and—his chief aim—as a successor to the Holy Chair. After the meetings of 1520, it seemed reasonably certain that Henry VIII would form an effective alliance with Charles V. Indeed, a treaty was made at Bruges and Calais in August and November 1521, but the ratification of military assistance was shelved until Charles should visit England—a visit which Wolsey tried his best to postpone as long as possible. Then came Charles's election as Emperor of the Holy Roman Empire and Wolsey's immediate concern became the maintenance of peace, while at the same time he had to see to it that no understanding should be reached between either Charles V and Francis I, or Francis and the Pope. As to the sudden treaty between the Pope and Charles, this had come into being, quite unforeseen, as a by-product of political improvisations in France.

In the astonishing welter of all these complicated dealings, Henry VIII enjoyed, entirely through Cardinal Wolsey's high competence, the triumph of having both Francis I and Charles V pay him visits at Calais, courting an alliance which he was not obliged to grant to either of them. The lasting result of such a diplomatic success was that the King's self-esteem increased enormously and that he regarded such a situation as perpetual and as quite normal, even in times when in actual fact he was absolutely isolated. Of this we shall see instances later on.

The foregoing summary of political affairs is of necessity
rather sketchy. Its purpose for our context is to demonstrate
that a firm alliance of any of the contesting parties with Henry
would have had decisive consequences, while it was precisely Wolsey's aim to keep anything of a definite nature at
bay and instead to preserve a delicate 'balance of power'
and perpetual uncertainty all round. It was, therefore, all the
more astonishing that Henry VIII, by issuing his book against
Luther, should support the Pope in no uncertain terms. No
other king of the period would have cared to make such a
personal and voluntary demonstration of devoted loyalty
just then.

As we have already mentioned, Henry's true motives are a
matter for conjecture, here as on frequent other occasions.
There cannot be any doubt, however, that his keen desire to
obtain a title from the Pope similar in quality to those pos-
sessed by the Kings of France and Spain played a prominent
part. As already mentioned, he had applied for such a title
some time earlier, in 1515–17, even then suggesting *Defensor
Fidei*. And now, in 1521, a fine opportunity presented itself
to please the Pope greatly. From the beginning Henry VIII
saw to it that it should be made very clear to the Pope that
he expected a title in reward for the book.

5

We have already quoted from the letter which Pace wrote to
Cardinal Wolsey on April 16th, 1521, in which he informed
him that the King was about to finish his treatise on Luther.
A few weeks afterwards, on May 21st, the King wrote to the
Pope, announcing his desire to dedicate to him 'the first
offerings of his intellect and his little erudition', by means of
which he had 'thought it right further to testify his zeal for
the faith by his writings, that all might see he was ready to
defend the church, not only with his arms, but with the re-
sources of his mind'.[25]

By July the book had been printed and beautifully bound
in cloth of gold, and in August it was forwarded to the English ambassador at Rome, Dr. Clerk. On August 25th Wolsey

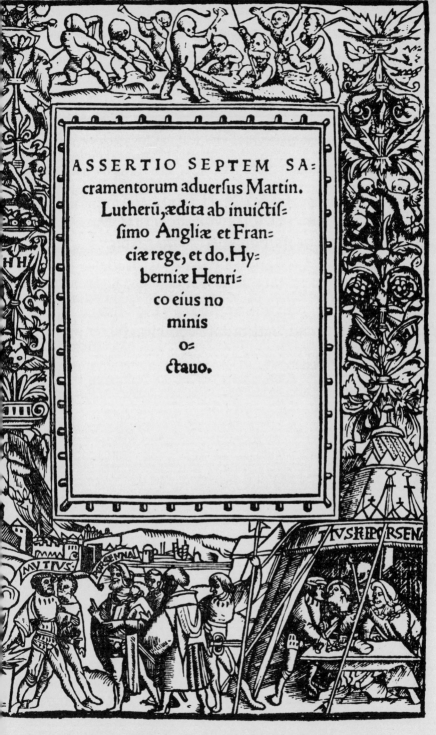

ASSERTIO SEPTEM SA=
cramentorum aduerſus Martin.
Lutherũ, ædita ab inuictiſ=
ſimo Angliæ et Fran=
ciæ rege, et do. Hy=
berniæ Henri=
co eius no
minis
o=
ctauo.

I and II. Henry VIII's book *Assertio Septem Sacramentorum*.
First edition (1521). Title page and (overleaf) advertisement of the
Papal Indulgence granted to the reader.

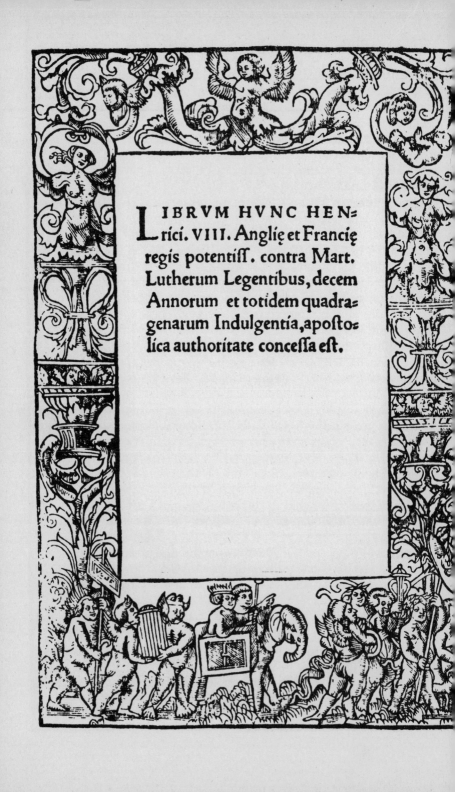

LIBRVM HVNC HEN=
rici. VIII. Anglię et Francię
regis potentiſſ. contra Mart.
Lutherum Legentibus, decem
Annorum et totidem quadra=
genarum Indulgentia, apoſto=
lica authoritate conceſſa eſt.

sent instructions to Clerk: he should make a careful study
of the King's prefatory epistle and proem and present the
book to the Pope with a solemn oration in which he should
conform his words to the contents of the book with such addi-
tions as he should think proper. In particular, Dr. Clerk was
instructed to declare that 'the King had styled himself the
very Defender of the Catholic Faith of Christ's Church,
which [title] he has truly deserved of the Apostolic See'.[26]

On September 15th Dr. Clerk presented the beautifully
produced volume to Leo X who read a few pages with great
delight and said the most flattering things about it. All the
same, there was one express wish of Henry's which the Pope
found it difficult to fulfil. Henry had requested the maximum
of spectacular ceremony for the presentation of the book, but
the Pope considered it advisable to avoid all excessive pomp
lest the laity might be reminded too strongly of the Lutheran
affair. Even Italy was not immune from influences; there had
been infiltrations of Lutheran sentiments such as in the case
of the friar Andrea of Ferrara who had threatened to publish
heretical propositions.[27] After intricate discussions with the
Pope in various private audiences, Dr. Clerk was assured of
the greatest display possible under existing circumstances;
he was to present the book early in October before a solemn
consistory of cardinals. In one of the later audiences, Clerk
reports, the Pope also 'demandyd of me, wherapon myne
Oracion shold most rest, to the intent he myght prepare me
an answer accordyngly'. Clerk replied that he 'cowd do no
lesse butt speke somwhat in the detestation of Leuther [sic]'
and otherwise of the King's great zeal for the Church and the
Holy See.[28]

There was one aspect of the final ceremonial arrangements
which perturbed Clerk personally; the master of ceremonies
requested of him 'amongst all other that I shold kneel apon
my knees all the tyme of myn Oracion. Wherat I was somwhat
abashyd for me thowght I shold nott have my harte ne my
spiritis so moche att my libertye. I fearyd greatly lest they
shold nott serve me so well kneelying as they wold stondyng.
How be it ther was no remedy. . . .'[29]

At last, on October 2nd, the ceremony took place. As was
requested of him Dr. Clerk's speech conformed largely to
Henry's own words. He began with a general denunciation

c

of Luther, culminating in references to the *Babylonian Captivity of the Church,* 'in which, good God! what and how prodigious poison, what deadly bain, how much consuming and mortal venom this poisonous serpent has spewed out . . . Here the bond of chastity is broken, holy fasts, religious vows, rites, ceremonies, worship of God, solemnity of the Mass etc. are abolished and exterminated, by the strangest perfidiousness that ever was heard of. This man institutes sacraments after his own fancy, reducing them to three, to two, to one; and that one he handles so pitifully that he seems about to reducing it at last to nothing at all. . . . When dreading punishment (which he well deserved) fled, with a mischief, into his perpetual lurking holes in Bohemia, the mother and nurse of his heresies. . . .'

Next, Dr. Clerk assured the Pope and the cardinals that there was no other nation which more condemned and detested Luther than England and then he arrived at the crux of the matter, his panegyric upon Henry VIII:

'I believe it will cause admiration in several that a prince so much busied with the cares of his own kingdom, both at home and abroad and whose affairs afford him so little respite, should undertake such things, as according to the common saying, might require to imploy wholly all the thoughts of a man, and indeed of such a one who is no novice either, but rather for his whole time experienced in the studies of learning. Yet notwithstanding all this, he that considers his great actions done for the faith of Christ and his accustomed reverence towards this Holy See, will not think it so strange that he, who with his forces and revenging sword has formerly defended the church of Rome when in greatest dangers and calamities of wars, should now for the glory of God and tranquillity of the Roman church, by his ingenuity and pen, put a stop to heresies which so endanger the Catholic faith. . . .

'I confess what the Godly Prince has writ against Luther's errors might compel Luther himself (if he had the least spark of Christian piety in him) to recant his heresies and recall again the straying and almost forlorn sheep. . . . But what can be done where Pharao's heart is hardened? Where the wound stinks with putrification? . . . Truly my most serene king is so far from expecting any good from this idol and vain phantom that he rather thinks this raging and mad dog is not to be dealt with by words. . . .'

Finally, Clerk emphasized the rather fine point that the King would only be willing to publish his book with the Pope's consent 'from whom we ought to receive the sense of the Gospel by your quick and most sublime judgment'.[30]

Clerk's report continues: 'after myn Oracion I rose vpe and with iij obeysaunce went vnto the pope and delyverd him the Kyng's booke'. This done he returned to his place, went down on his knees again and the Pope delivered his reply.[31] Clerk listened with the greatest attention to catch all possible finer points. He had also given special instructions to two of his attendants to listen with equal care so that the three could afterwards compare their impressions of the Pope's speech.

The Pope's reply was, as may be expected, most flattering and full of praise for Henry VIII that he, 'having the knowledge, will and ability of composing this book against this terrible monster, has rendered himself no less admirable to the whole world by the eloquence of his style and by his great wisdom. We render immortal thanks to our creator who has raised such a prince to defend His Holy Church and this Holy See. . . .'[32]

The Pope also granted an indulgence of ten years and ten quadragenes to those who would read the King's book or listen to its content.

There followed a revival of the old discussions of 1515–16 as to which title might be most appropriate for the King of England, in the course of which Henry VIII might well have become the 'most orthodox', or even the 'angelic' king. In the end, however, Henry's own preference and often communicated desire won the day and it was the title *Defensor Fidei* which was conferred upon him.[33]

Cardinal Wolsey soon thanked Clerk in the King's name for all he had achieved but he still reminded him that 'necesary it is ye diligently procure and solicite that not ovnely suche ample and sufficient bulles and loving brieves as shal be requisite for the said Title be incontinently sped and with velerite sent vnto the kings Grace, if it not alredy don bifore thys tyme', and that all remaining copies of the King's book should be sent to universities and princes, together with the Pope's bull of approbation.[34]

Actually, there was no cause for anxiety: the bull confirming the title was promptly sent to Cardinal Wolsey who surrendered it to the King in a spectacular assembly at Greenwich; there followed a solemn Mass sung by Wolsey and assisted by the Earl of Essex and the Dukes of Suffolk and Norfolk. After the blessing, the bull was 'eftsones declared, and trumpettes blew, the shalmes and sagbuttes plaied in honor of the kynges new style. Thus hys hyghnes went to dinner. In the middes whereof, the kyng of Heraldes and his compaignie began the larges, criying *Henricus dei gratia rex Angliae, et Franciae, defensor fidei, et dominus Hiberniae,* thus ended the dinner, with much hubandance of vitaill and wyne, to all manner of people.'[35]

Henry VIII was delighted to see a long-cherished desire fulfilled and it seems that it was not immediately noticed that his title was, after all, somewhat inferior to the titles conferred upon the Kings of France and Spain: it was not hereditary. Even the corrected confirmation of the title which Henry requested and obtained from Clement VII only contained the ambiguous word *perpetuum.* Inasmuch as it was the custom clearly to specify a hereditary title as such, the uncertain formulation of the confirmation seems to indicate that a definite clarification of the point was studiously avoided. However, there came a time when Henry VIII could attend to such matters without making petitions: in 1543 an Act of Parliament made the papal title hereditary.[36] At Rome, Henry's title had been revoked in a bull of Paul III in 1535; almost immediately, the bull was suspended, but in 1538 it was made definite.

6

Henry VIII's book against Luther bears the title *Assertio Septem Sacramentorum,* and maintains that Luther was a vile heretic whose false and frivolous teaching was the fruit of a mind utterly divorced from God. Despite Luther's immeasurable arrogance, his heresy was nothing but empty wind. The King predicted that soon Luther would deny the presence of the Body and Blood of Christ in the Sacrament of the Altar and that he would soon dispense with the Sacrament of Holy Baptism as well. He would not, Henry wrote, attempt to bring about a recantation from Luther by means of his book, as the case seemed hopeless. 'Alas! The most greedy wolf of hell has surprised him, devoured and swallowed him down into the lowest part of his belly where he lies half alive, and half in death. And whilst the pious Pastor calls him and bewails his loss, he belches out of the filthy mouth of the hellish wolf these foul inveighings which the ears of the whole flock do detest, disdain and abhor.'

Various estimates have been given regarding the quality of Henry's work. Father O'Donovan, when issuing in 1908 a reprint of Thomas Webster's English translation of 1687, wrote a lengthy preface and assessed the significance of the book so highly that he gave expression to his hope that Anglican readers of Henry's arguments might be called back to the Roman obedience. Such praise of the book is unqualified to the point of absurdity.

There are other opinions. J. Pratt, the editor of Foxe's *Actes and Monuments*, laconically calls Henry's book 'this curious production';[37] this seems a little inadequate. Burnet wrote: 'this book was magnified by the clergy as the most learned work that ever the sun saw; and he was compared with King Solomon. . . . It must be acknowledged that, considering the age, and that it was the work of a king, it did deserve some commendation.'[38] Brewer judges: 'it produced without novelty or energy the old commonplaces of authority, tradition and general consent. The cardinal principles of Luther's teaching the king did not understand and did not therefore attempt to refute. Contented to point out the mere straws on the surface of the current . . . reproduces without force, originality or feeling the weary topics he had picked up, without much thought or research, from the theological manuals of the day.'[39] On the other hand, again, Philip Hughes defines the King's book as 'a remarkable production . . . a great success . . . a correction of the prophet's theological howlers'.[40]

Wider still is the variety of opinions relating to the actual authorship. There are not many historians who believe that

Henry wrote the book unaided. The chief advocate for this rarely represented theory is Father O'Donovan who, in the preface to his edition of the text, took great trouble to demonstrate that the King was the sole, unaided author; among his points of proof, Henry's own assurance and the corroboration of Erasmus rank high. The latter made mention of the King's book in two letters of August 23rd, 1521. To Pace he wrote about it in terms of conventional flattery such as were not intended to be taken as a statement of true, critical conviction, and to Archbishop Warham he wrote that, from what he had heard from Mountjoy and others, he was convinced that the book was the King's own. Hallam thought that the book might have been Henry's own work but that he must have had help with the Latin; T. E. Bridgett concurs with this opinion.

There are others who believe that Henry VIII was not the author at all. Foxe wrote: 'This book, albeit it carries the king's name in the title, yet it was another that ministered the motion, another that framed the style. But whosoever had the labour of this book, the king had the thanks and also the reward.'[41] Burnet wrote: 'No doubt this book was wrote by the king as other books were under his name: that is, by his bishops or other learned men.'[42] It has been suggested that Cardinal Wolsey or Bishop John Fisher or Richard Pace had helped or, indeed, written the book. Such discussions were already current among contemporaries. Poor Erasmus! In Germany he was under the suspicion of having written the King's book against Luther and in England he was suspected of being the author of Luther's vitriolic reply to Henry VIII. He sighed: 'If only they would change sides, that is, if only the English suspected what the Germans suspect!' As late as 1523 he was under this cloud and wrote an anxious, assuring letter to Bishop Tunstall. Luther was somehow firmly convinced that Edward Lee was the true author of Henry's book.

Since Henry VIII was certainly not entirely ignorant of theological matters, and inspired his contemporaries to applaud his great learning in ever-repeated flattery, it seems unlikely that he should not have done a good deal of the writing himself. Whether or not Lord Herbert was right in presuming that Henry was originally destined for a clerical career, the King certainly had had an uncommonly good education. On the other hand, he had never studied theology methodically and it seems therefore highly unlikely that the final version of the book should have been his own and not the work of a schooled cleric. The question of the authorship will probably remain obscure. There is little one can add to the chorus of opinions: 'Mr. Brewer seems to believe the book to have been written by Henry because it is so bad. The Bishop of La Rochelle, who wrote an introduction to the French edition of 1850, considers it impossible that he could have produced the work because it is so good. Horace Walpole pronounces the book a bad one, and yet too good for a king to have written.'[43]

7

If it was Henry VIII's primary aim to gain the papal title *Defensor Fidei* in reward for the book, then it was worth the effort. If, however, his genuine concern was to correct Luther, the book can hardly be said to have achieved its purpose. By 1521 the divergence of Luther's approach to theological inquiry from the prevalent post-scholastic routine procedure of thought was fully established. If the book was indeed Henry's own, the mere compilation of the arguments it contains was certainly some achievement. However, Luther was well acquainted with the basic traditional precepts which he regarded critically as either tenable, or else as unobligatory at best, and as erroneous at worst. He could not possibly have been expected to be disturbed, or in the least influenced, by the King's assembly of familiar, elementary statements. It was customary at that time for opponents to accuse one another of abysmal ignorance, but if any of the attacks upon Luther underestimated the latter's range of knowledge, it was certainly Henry's book. There were others in England who took a more realistic view. Nicholas Wilson's letters prefixed to the Latin edition of Fisher's sermon preached against Luther at St. Paul's Cross maintained that Luther was a very learned man and that he would have been a great ornament to the Church of Christ if his innocence had equalled his learning.[44] Whatever one's personal opinion of Luther's status may be, it can surely be assumed that as a theologian he was Henry VIII's equal. Of course, we may presume with even greater certainty that Henry VIII was unaware of it.

In conclusion, the King's book was neither much better nor much worse than many another elaboration of its kind. The controversial literature of the period provides ample evidence that Luther was a favourite target for inadequate attacks. But, compared with the anti-Lutheran writings of John Faber, the *Assertio Septem Sacramentorum* appears to lack all significance. It is entirely due to the author's name that the book is not forgotten by posterity quite so completely as are the excited tracts of Eck or Cochlaeus.

What then is the significance of Henry VIII's book apart from the King's success in securing the long-coveted title? As far as the future of Lutheran influence in England was concerned, its real significance seems to rest upon the fact that Luther wrote a reply of such scathing lack of respect— considering he was addressing a king—that it was natural for Henry VIII to regard him as an impossible person for a very long time. I do not think, however, that one of the chief results of either the King's book or of Luther's rejoinder was that 'it made all personal contact with Luther impossible'.[45] Only ten years later Henry VIII showed the most determined eagerness to gain a friendly gesture from Luther.

From the Pope's point of view, the book's significance was quite inestimable. As I have already remarked, no other prince would have cared during those times of uncertainty to give so formidable a proof of profound devotion and personal loyalty as Henry VIII demonstrated with the *Assertio*. Nothing can serve better to illustrate how remarkable was the demonstration than the reaction of Sir Thomas More, who warned the King that it might be unwise to write quite so warmly. This referred to statements in the King's book such as the following: 'I will not wrong the bishop of Rome so much as troublesomely or carefully to dispute his right as if it were a matter doubtful.... All the faithful honour and acknowledge the Sacred Roman See for their mother and supreme; nor does distance of place or dangers in the way hinder access thereto.... How could he [i.e. Luther] expect, I say, that anybody should believe (as I know not as he could desire they should) that all nations, cities, nay kingdoms and provinces should be so prodigal of their rights and liberties as to acknowledge the superiority of a strange priest to whom they should owe no subjection?'

After many years, More remembered all this well and said, according to Roper: 'When I founde the pope's aucthority highly advaunced and with stronge argumentes mightlye defended, I said vnto his grace: "I must put your highnes in remembraunce of one thinge, and that is this. The pope, as your grace knowethe, is a prince as you are, and in league with all other Christian princes. It may hereafter so fall owte that your grace and he may varye vppon some pointes of the league wherevppon may grow breach of amitye and warre betweene you bothe. I thinke it best, therefore, that the place be amended and his aucthority more sclenderly touched." "Nay," quoth his grace, "that it shall not, we are so much bounden to the See of Rome that we can not do too muche honor vnto it." '[46]

As we know, a time came when Henry VIII changed his mind in matters relating to the concept of supremacy in the Church and that the most illustrious martyr to that particular royal change of mind was none other than the person who had foreseen trouble, though probably in a less drastic form —Sir Thomas More.

It was a grave decision in the early sixteenth century for a prince to break all spiritual allegiance to Rome, even as late as 1533 when Henry VIII effected the separation. He was then, of course, well aware that precedents had been successful, that he was by no means the first and that the risk involved was therefore infinitesimally smaller in 1533 than it had been in 1520. However that may be, one cannot ignore the fact that no other prince with a Protestant future had ever volunteered such enthusiastic declarations of unshakeable loyalty to the Pope and that, therefore, the impression of scandalous faithlessness made by Henry VIII was incomparably stronger than that made by any other Protestant prince. And here we do not even take into account the motive which caused the breach.

Lastly, the significance of the King's book rests upon the undoubted fact that he remained determined to maintain the validity of all seven sacraments even at a time when he was trying hard to ingratiate the Lutherans in order to become a

member, indeed the leader, of the Schmalkald League of the
German Protestant princes. There was the one notable exception of the *Ten Articles* of 1536 which mentioned only
three sacraments; they were soon revoked. But for this
quickly passing episode, Henry VIII never compromised in
asserting the seven sacraments. It is satisfying to record at
least one instance of consistency in the progress of this king.

8

From its beginning, the Lutheran reformation brought about,
as a by-product, a prolific literature of controversial tracts,
extending from the smallest pamphlets to incredibly large
tomes. These varied, as they were bound to do, in intrinsic
value. While some of this vast literature helped Luther towards ever clearer formulations, there was no one of his own
stature among those who opposed him. It is therefore not
difficult to imagine the excitement among these mediocrities
when no less a person than the King of England joined the
ranks of the anti-Lutheran writers. Henry VIII's book appeared in two German translations in 1522, one made by
Hieronymus Emser, the other by Thomas Murner.

Emser's translation[47] was made at the request of Duke
George of Saxony and dedicated to Duchess Barbara. In his
long dedicatory preface Emser wrote: 'Nobody has protected
our Holy Faith, the Mass, Indulgences and all other [*sic*]
sacraments so powerfully and defended them so masterly
against Luther as the King of England. Wherefore His Holiness the Pope has issued a special Bull bestowing upon him
and his descendants the new title of defender of the faith and
has granted an indulgence of ten years and of the same number of quadragenes to all the faithful who read this book or
listen to its contents. This should surely attract your Serene
Highness and all pious Christian hearts to read the book diligently, as all the world and every person concerned with the
faith and with the salvation of his soul is deeply affected by
these matters. . . .'

Thomas Murner produced his translation at Strasbourg
under his own initiative. Only a short while before he had

published a German translation of Luther's *De Captivitate Babylonica Ecclesiae*, the very book chosen by Henry VIII for his attack upon the reformer, and it seems that at the time he was impressed by Luther's argument; like so many others, he was opposed to Luther after an initial period of non-committal sympathy with Luther's presumed broader aims.

The two translations of the King's book created much excitement and induced Luther to write a reply immediately. His Latin answer *Contra Henricum Regem Angliae* was followed by a German version of his own which was not a translation, strictly speaking, differing as it does from the Latin book in numerous minor details.

On December 13th, 1522, Hannibal wrote to Wolsey about this reply: 'Luther has of late written agenst the Kings Grace; whych Book I send to you: the book is full of raylinge agenst the Kyngs Grace. I soght all Rome to know whether wer mor, bot I coude fynde non. If any mo cumme, the Pope has comandyde that non shall cumme in lyght. I shall take them all, and pay for them and brent them.'[48]

As we have already remarked in an earlier context, one of the outstanding characteristics of Luther's answer is its excessive rudeness. The prolific insults and outbursts of invective tend perhaps to obscure the fact that actually the reply provided a competent rejection of the King's commonplaces from his, the Lutheran, point of view. The abuse is very frequently too strong to be excusable, considering that Luther was addressing a king, but, on the other hand, it is not difficult to understand that Luther should feel some impatience with the excitement about so ill-informed and shallow an attack from so illustrious a quarter. Throughout his reply, one of Luther's chief complaints was that the author of the *Assertio Septem Sacramentorum*, like all his adversaries, had failed to understand, or had chosen to ignore, the fundamental distinction made by him between sound teaching based upon the Scriptures, on the one hand, and the apparatus of tradition, customs, decretals and scholastic decisions or opinions, on the other.

Luther's reply to Henry VIII begins:

'Our Lord Jesus Christ has smitten the whole realm of papal abomination with blindness and madness. For three years now, the mad giants have been struggling against Luther and they still do not grasp what my fight with them is all about. It seems, in vain have I published so many writings which testify openly that I seek to demonstrate that Scripture should count as the exclusive authority, as is right and fair; that human contrivances and doctrines should be given up as evil scandals or, at least, that once their poison is extracted (that is, the power to enforce them and to make them obligatory for the conscience), they should be regarded as a matter for free investigation just as any other calamity or plague in the world. Because they fail to understand this, they quote against me exclusively man-made laws, glosses on the writings of the fathers and from the history of old customs, in short: precisely what I reject and what I am contesting. They themselves know very well that all those things are unreliable and that frequently they contain errors. My struggle concerns principles, they answer stressing usage and custom. I ask: "By what authority do you do this?" They answer: "*Because* we are doing it, and have always done so." Instead of discussing the basic cause, they discuss intentions instead of Scripture, usages instead of my principal concern, custom—and all this in things pertaining to God!

'They have in their schools a questionable method in disputations, called the repetition of the question (i.e. reverting to the point under dispute). Thus, they study and teach until they turn grey—right to their grave—with endless labour and at great cost, the miserable men. They themselves cannot do anything else with their teaching, it is the only way they can dispute. And that is the reason why it happens that, if I always cry: "Gospel! Gospel! Gospel!", they can only answer: "Fathers! Fathers! Custom! Custom! Decretals! Decretals!" If then I answer that customs, fathers and decretals have often erred, that reform must be based upon sounder foundation because Christ cannot err, then they are silent like the fishes, or as the Scripture says: "Like deaf adders they stop their ears, lest they should hear the voice of the charmer." '

Another point which Luther deeply resented was Henry VIII's charge that he was inconsistent, a charge frequently raised by the anti-Lutheran pamphleteers. This had already become a standard reproach; invariably, the method chosen was to demonstrate that there were several things which Luther had still considered acceptable or defensible in 1517 whereas he rejected them entirely in 1521, and then to deduct that clearly Luther did not know his own mind. Sir Thomas More's *Dialogue concerning Tyndale* does not fail to repeat the accusation after the usual pattern. On this point, Luther replied to Henry VIII:

'... He condemns me as writing contradictory statements and as being in contradiction with myself. Here the miserable scribbler, lacking proper substance, has demonstrated with poisonous words how well he can manage to soil a lot of paper, a truly royal deed! How far he was justified in writing all that, the reader will be able to deduct from the fact that the secretive Thomist did not quote a single instance as an example to prove my inconsistency. The boasting king simply performs a trick of rhetorics: Luther is inconsistent—who, therefore, can believe him? That is quite enough for the new defender of the church, for this deity newly arrived in England. To quote an example was unnecessary. Luther must not be given an opportunity to clear himself and to deal with the foolish king according to Thomistic dignity.'

The passage in Henry VIII's book reads:

'What avails it to dispute against one, who disagrees with everyone, even with himself? Who affirms in one place what he denies in another; denying what he presently affirms. Who if you object faith, combats by reason; if you touch him with reason, pretends faith. If you allege philosophers, he flies to scriptures; if you propound scriptures, he trifles with sophistry....'

Regarding the 'contradictions' between his earlier and the later writings, Luther writes (in the German version of his answer to Henry): 'From now on, no Christian can any longer improve himself or do penance, because the King of England would come along and say: "Look! They confess as sin and error what formerly they maintained to be good and right...." I wonder whether so clever a king keeps wearing his children shoes which, after all, are a contradiction of the shoes a grown man uses? How can he nowadays drink wine, considering there was a time when he was sucking milk?'

Luther's answer then proceeds to explain once again his fundamental distinction between scriptural concepts such as faith, good works, charity, repentance and so forth, and concepts unknown in the Scriptures such as the papacy, decisions of councils, indulgences, purgatory, the Mass, monastic vows and so forth. As regards the first category, Luther maintained that he had never changed his opinions, that he had only developed them; as to the second group, he had only gradually come to see, with the help of those who defended them against his criticism, that they were not merely unbiblical but actually anti-biblical.

In reply to the King's argument that the doctrines rejected by Luther had been believed for a very long time and that it was inconceivable that so many should have been deceived, Luther replied that he did not ask how long doctrines had been in existence, but by what right they were sustained; also the faith of the Turks was about a thousand years old and the pagans had a still older faith and that they numbered ten times more than the Christians—how could one reject them if Henry's argument was to the point? What infuriated Luther more than anything else in the King's book, however, was the author's implicit ignorance of his true teaching.

'In addition to the products of all the other madmen, this new god has brought a new, peculiar folly to the market ... He says openly that he will leave my principal argument undiscussed—others could deal with that—and only wishes to attack my resolutions ... "I will prove that there are seven sacraments but I will leave undiscussed the main reasoning of my opponent"—what a fool, that he believes one could conduct a disputation in such a fashion! One might suppose that a declared enemy of the king had written the book to bring everlasting disgrace upon him. ...'

9

As Luther was replying to an attack which had entirely failed to open new vistas, there is nothing in his answer that he had not said or written before. It seems desirable, however, to return to the question of Luther's excessive rudeness. His apologists have sometimes proposed that it was intended to stress his firm conviction that the book had not been written by the King himself. This seems untenable. Although Luther expressed the opinion that Edward Lee was the most likely true author, he made it quite clear that he had resolved to ignore the question of the true authorship: 'It does not concern me that no one believes the book to have been written by him. I take it for the king's under whose name it has been published; I will direct my attack against the foolish king who suffered fools to misuse his name.'

Now, whatever can, and must, be said about the unnecessarily objectionable language in which Luther addressed Henry VIII, this must be judged in its proper perspective. There has hardly ever been a time in which slogans and abusive verbosity, frequently childishly primitive, were so widespread and in common use as in the sixteenth century. Firstly, slogans: words which look to us quite harmless were considered unforgivable insults, such as *sophist, Thomist, summist, theologist, romanist*, and so forth. When, through overuse, the novelty had worn off, it was for a time sufficient to reheat the insult by means of the prefix 'arch-'; *archsophist, archthomist*, etc. Next came invective such as 'murderer of souls, dog, swine, adder' and the like. Highly popular were puns with an abusive intent. To Luther, his opponent Dr. Eck became the contraction 'Dreck', the German term for dirt. Luther's name attracted Sir Thomas More's alliteration 'lowsy Luther'. A 'romanist', disliking to see himself called 'popish', found relief in his exasperation by calling the others 'martinish'. Everybody was busily engaged in the search for new phrases. Cochlaeus—to Luther 'Kochloeffel' (i.e. kitchen spoon)—wrote of 'our bombastic Luther-preachers and Scripture-johnnies'. One Bachmann wrote a tract entitled *A Little Handkerchief for Luther's Spittle*. The 'Martinists' called the 'papists' 'chalice thieves' because they permitted communion only in one kind. Everybody was to everybody else a 'schismaticus', a 'church-splitter' and, of course, opponents were invariably 'poisonous'. On rare occasions, someone was really witty in this endless game of abuse, but usually a poor play with words, coarse abuse and infinite repetition of boring slogans sufficed to keep all tempers hot.

Henry VIII too, no less than Luther, wrote one or two phrases which go far beyond the modern reader's ideas of polite, not to mention royal, intercourse. His references to Luther include 'a venomous serpent, a pernicious plague, infernal wolf, cerberus-like, an infectious soul, a detestable trumpeter of pride, calumnies and schism, having an execrable mind, a filthy tongue, a detestable touch, stuffed with venom, this hideous monster being catch'd will become benumbed and pine away by his own vermin . . .' In a letter to Charles V of May 20th, 1521, Henry VIII wrote of Luther as 'this weed, this dilapidated, sick and evilminded sheep'.

Vocabulary of this kind was the normal tool of controversy and not at all a Lutheran monopoly. In fact, it would have been surprising if either Henry VIII or Luther had conducted the controversy in the modern manner, formulating their attack, or their rejoinder to an attack, in deliberate and exquisite courtesy in order to render it devastating. In the sixteenth century the weapon of politeness was reserved for the last extremity, as can be demonstrated by the titles of successive controversial booklets exchanged between Luther and Emser during the years 1520 and 1521:

I   *Emser against the unchristian Book of Martin Luther, Augustinian, to the German Nobility*

II   *Luther to the Sheep at Leipzig* (N.B. Emser's coat of arms depicted a ram)

III   *To the Bull at Wittenberg*

IV   *In Reply to the Sheep's Answer*

V   *Answer to the Wittenberg Bull's furious Rejoinder*

VI   *Reply to the super-christian, super-spiritual, super-artful Book of Sheep Emser of Leipzig*

And so this went on for a while until, at last, Luther wrote a missive entitled *Luther to the reverend, learned Priest of God, Herr H. Emser, Vicarius at Meissen.* Emser continued to write against Luther, but the latter no longer deemed him worthy of a reply; the formal, polite address on his last book against Emser was nothing else but the expression of unspeakable contempt. It may well be that Luther could not have dared to address the King of England in controversy with an ice-cold politeness as this might have been con-

CONTRA HENRICVM
REGEM ANGLIAE
MARTINVS LV.
THER.

VVUTTEMBERGAE.
1522.

III. Luther's reply to Henry VIII's book, Latin version, (1522).
Title page.

sidered the worst imaginable affront. Neverthless, there could
have been a little restraint.

As soon as Henry VIII's *Assertio* had been published in
German, Luther was determined not to mince words but to
pay back in kind, with interest. To Spalatinus he wrote: 'I
have written so sharply against the erroneous bishops with
full intention and I shall be equally tough in the contest with
the King of England.' His reply to Henry VIII ends with this
statement:

'In conclusion, if my severity and violence towards the
king offends anyone, let him hear this reply: in this book I
am dealing with senseless, wild monsters who have despised
whatever I have written calmly and in a moderate tone. . . .
Anyway, at least I have abstained from poisonous slanders
and lies such as abound in the king's book. Actually, it is of
little consequence if I despise and bite some earthly king,
considering that he did not hesitate to blaspheme against
the King in Heaven and to commit sacrilege with his poisonous lies. The Lord judges the nations in righteousness,
Amen.'

Although, as we have shown, abuse and invective could
be taken for granted in all controversial writings of the time,
contemporary reaction to Luther's answer reveals that in this
particular case some moderation was considered fitting. Not
only were Luther's antagonists scandalized—that could be
interpreted in various ways—but a number of Luther's close
friends were sufficiently puzzled to write to Luther on the
matter. Luther's replies to such letters show that he was
quite unrepentant. To an unnamed correspondent he replied:[49]

'You wish to know the reasons why I gave so hard an
answer to the King of England. In order to enable you to give
answer to my opponents, I will tell you that I have done it
after careful deliberation. From now on I will no longer deal
gently with slanderers and liars. My preaching and writing
has reached a limit.

'You know that Christ, Peter and Paul were not always
gentle. How often does He call the Jews "snakes, murderers,
children of the devil, fools . . ." [Luther gives further ex-

D

amples.] Now, as you know, I have written many a kindly
book without any rudeness, friendly and gentle, abounding in
humility. I have run after them, I appeared in person at much
cost and strain and I have suffered their lies and slanders
beyond all reasonable measure. But the more I humbled myself, the more they stormed against me and my teaching, because they can neither hear nor see.

'Those who have never taken any notice of my patience
and submission or those who despised me on account of them,
may now be furious about my railing. Why should I worry?
It only goes to show that they do not recognize anything
good in me; they only look for good reasons to belittle me.
A man who regards my teaching with a kind heart would
not be offended with my admonitions.

'Does it not expose their wrong judgment that they refuse
to take notice of the railing and slanders of my opponents,
considering that they praise them as being the finest Christians and regard me as a heretic? Actually they have done
much more railing than I and they did it in whole formations
against me who stood alone. Judge for yourself what kind of
people they are who ignore whatever is acceptable in me
and only take hold of rudeness. However, as I have said, let
God's judgment begin, so that all take offence and fall away
who are not worthy of Him, just as (John vi, 60) many of
Christ's disciples ran away, saying: "The saying is too hard,
who can hear it?"

'Therefore, my dear friend, be not astonished that many
are scandalized by my writings. It shall be so and it must be
so that only few stay with the Gospel. And the Gospel hates
no man more than one with a false heart who is a friend only
until, a little later, things begin to look a bit sour, and then
they fall away. How could such a man stake his life if the
hour or persecution demand it?

'*Summa*, time will show why it is that I must be so hard.
Whosoever will not believe that it is done from a good heart
and that it is well done, let him leave it; a time will surely
come when he will be forced to see it clearly. My gracious
lord, too, and many other friends have written to admonish
me. But my answer is invariably that I will not, that I must
not leave it. My business is not that of a middle-man who
can give in a little, reduce a little or withdraw altogether, as

I have done hitherto, fool that I am. Herewith I commend you to God.

Martin Luther.'

10

Henry VIII did not write a reply to Luther's answer. Refutations were written by Bishop John Fisher and Sir Thomas More. The Bishop's reply was calmly written but, seen quite objectively, lacked incisive strength in the theological argument, a defect aggravated by the diffusive length of the rejoinder. Sir Thomas More wrote in the abusively controversial fashion[50] under the pen-name of G. Rossaeus. For a long time the true identity of 'William Ross' remained unknown and More himself seems to have guarded the secret with some care; the book was written in 1523, and in the *Dialogue concerning Tyndale* of 1528 More still referred to 'William Ross' as to another person.

Historians and biographers who choose to refer to the rudeness in Luther's controversial writings as to a quite isolated instance of its kind, illustrating the deplorable depravity of the reformer, can hardly be expected to quote the invective contained in Henry VIII's *Assertio Septem Sacramentorum*. More's book against Luther seems to embarrass them considerably: here the abusive tone is so dominant and gross that it cannot be ignored or glossed over. The excesses are either deeply regretted, or far-fetched explanations are attempted. Frequently it is said that Sir Thomas More chose to amuse himself in the stylistic exercise of imitating the famous 'Lutheran' rudeness. Certainly the language is quite unrestrained, and Erasmus, one of the few who were absolutely opposed to such riots, was horrified and thought that 'Rossaeus' (he was, of course, unaware that he had been reading a book by his friend More) was far worse even than Luther.[51]

Erasmus's antipathy to the polemical technique of his time is a reaction not to be equated with the prudish embarrassment of modern historians with a certain bias, or of apologists; his primary aim was to preserve his cherished, delicate neutrality in the chief issue of his time, his highest *desideratum* was peace. Those historians who choose to react with exaggerated accusation to Luther's rudeness and with regretful or pointless apologies to More's, do so in the service of partiality. Luther, as I have said, might have restrained himself somewhat since he was addressing the King of England. There was no reason whatever for Sir Thomas More, in writing against Luther, to refrain from making unrestrained use of the conventional armament of strongest malice. To be sure, he may well have enjoyed, as all controversialists do, the stylistic pleasures of coining crashing phrases, new and witty. As distinct from the multitude of mediocre scribblers of the age—how many there were!—who were restricted to the dull repetition of lame, outworn slogans, he was, after all, nearly as inventive and witty in foul language as Luther could be on grand occasions. While the poor mediocrities revelled in their lame repetitions, he could write, for instance, of the Lutherans as of those who have as much shame in their faces as a shotten herring has shrimps in her tail. It would have been excellent if More had consistently displayed a racy wit of this kind. In fact, this is not the case. His controversial writings against Tyndale contain a lot of abusive verbiage, particularly those tiresome series of adjectives, which fail to improve on the invective of lesser writers.

It was not only insult and abuse in style which served to show that a writer was earnestly determined to hurt his opponent. A good controversialist had also to be prolific in the invention of new accusations. These need not be true, but they had to be really shocking. They came in as a useful weapon when confronted with arguments which were difficult to answer on a more factual level. Sir Thomas More's main source of information about Lutheran affairs in Germany was Johann Cochlaeus.* Even so, there is no reason to believe that he was truly convinced that every day at Wittenberg was given up to bacchanalian festivities, but was not the

---

* The role of Cochlaeus as disseminator of hair-raising stories about the life of the Lutherans, and particularly of Luther himself, continued even at a time when his name was practically forgotten. His *Commentaria de Actis et Scriptis M. Lutheri* served as an arsenal for anti-Lutheran writers; long after the original ceased to be consulted, the stories were kept alive by means of endless repetition and the influence can be traced right down to modern times. The *Commentaria* themselves only attained three editions in the sixteenth century and have not been printed since.

allegation a good, strong contrast to the observance of religious fasts which Luther deprecated? Upholding the principle
of celibacy for priests and the religious, More scored an extra
blow against the Lutherans by asserting that they had now
actually begun to establish polygamy. Having rejected
images, More wrote, the Lutherans now carry Luther's image
in solemn procession and offer it their veneration. Luther and
some pastors among his followers having married, More was
inspired to describe them as 'these bridegrooms, first sunk
deep in infamy, then ruined with disease and want, giving
themselves up to robbery. . . .'

Whether the authors of such lively nonsense be Lutheran,
Catholic or humanist, heretic, king or saint—they were of
their age, not of ours. Compared with the refined methods of
infamy in our modern age, their technique was primitive.
This is all we can say, if we wish to moralize.

11

In Germany, Luther's reply to Henry VIII's book provoked
the Franciscan, Thomas Murner, who had translated the
Assertio Septem Sacramentorum in 1522, to write in defence
of the King (*Defensio Libri Henrici Octavi Regis Angliae
contra Lutherum*).

Murner's career was interesting. He was born in 1475, became a Franciscan at Strasbourg in 1490, Doctor of Theology
at Freiburg in 1506, Doctor of Law at Basel in 1519. In 1526
he fled from Strasbourg, then a stronghold of the Reformation, to Lucerne where he became a parish priest. Here he
found himself again involved in the religious struggles and
had to go, returning to Alsace where he became a parish
priest at Oberehnheim. He was well known as a preacher, as
a translator (Virgil, 1515) and as the author of books on logic
and law. His more lasting fame, however, was established not
by his scholarly achievements but by his satirical poems, particularly by the *Narrenbeschwörung* of 1512. This latter work
was strongly influenced by Sebastian Brant's *Narrenschiff*
(Ship of Fools) from which Murner had helped himself to
whole sections for his versification, much as Alexander

Barclay and Watson had done in England in 1509. The book's
subject and concern were human folly of all sorts and, more
particularly, the exposition of ecclesiastical abuse. Originally Murner was in sympathy with Luther, but on seeing that
Luther went further than merely rectifying what was generally recognized as stark abuse, he began to write against the
reformer, first in a respectful tone but later more and more
polemically.

In 1523 Murner wrote a booklet in German under the title
Whether the King of England or Luther be a Liar.[52] The King
had, as may be remembered, attacked Luther with the charge
of inconsistency, a charge which Luther had rejected as a lie.
Murner's booklet undertakes an 'investigation' of the point.
Its form bears a superficial resemblance to the disputation: it
is written in the form of a dialogue between Henry VIII and
Luther and each exchange is followed by Murner's judicial
comment. In the preface Murner extols the King's merits:
'... who with his sword and reasoning protects Christendom
and to his immortal fame has done a supreme service to all
Christendom by his masterly book, just as if it were his desire
to look after the body, honour, goods and souls of us Germans ...' Murner also reveals from the outset the aim of his
book, 'that henceforth the heretic and run-away friar and
murderous bloodhound should keep quiet, who desires to
wash his hands in the blood of priests'.

The controversial strength of the book was its form, the
apparently unbiased objectivity in the confrontation of the
opponents. This, however, was by no means a new idea of
Murner's. Quite a number of controversial books of the time
were written in the form of a dialogue and nobody could be
expected to be ignorant of the trick. A really fair representa-
tion of the opponent was not intended and the outcome of the
contest was, of course, inevitable. The *Quod he*, as Tyndale
sarcastically calls Sir Thomas More's conversation partner in
the *Dialogue* concerning himself, was invariably quite easily
put to confusion; he was not, of course, allowed to say anything that could not be readily disposed of. It would not
have occurred to the writers of such dialogues that unwittingly they paid handsome compliments to their opponents
by reducing them to the stature of a poorly equipped *Quod
he.* An additional weakness of Murner's book lay in the fact

that the author was not really a passionate defender of his
chosen cause and that he had never taken up a clear position
theologically. In this respect he reminds us of Erasmus,
although quite clearly he was far from being at all compar-
able with Erasmus in either learning or style.

Murner's book was sent to Cardinal Wolsey by Hannibal
on May 5th, 1523.[53] Soon afterwards, Murner came to England through the inducement of an unknown person. On
August 26th, 1523, Sir Thomas More wrote to Wolsey: '... Hit
may ferther lyke yoʳ good grace to be advertised that one
Thomas Murner ffrere of sayn ffransisce order which wrote a
boke agaynst Luther in defence of the kinges boke was owte
of Almaigne sent in to Engl by the meane of a simple person
an almaign namying hymselfe seruant un to the kinges grace
& affermyng vn to Murner that the king had gevyn hym in
charge to desire Murner to cum to hym in to E(ngland) and
by the occasion thereof he is cumen over & hath n(ow) bene
here a good while. Wherefor the kinges grace pitiyng that he
was so deceived & having tendre respects to the good zele
he bereth toward the ffeith & his good hart & mind toward
his hignes requyreth yoʳ grace that it may lyke you to caus
him haue inreward one hundred pownde and that he may
retourne home. ...' The letter further informs the Cardinal
that the same 'simple person' had also brought over a German
baron's son on a fool's errand and that 'the kinges grace
greatly merveileth' about so many unbidden visitors.[54] In
order to save Murner embarrassment, the King gave him a
letter, addressed to the town councillors of Strasbourg, in
which he generously described Murner's journey as the
outcome of his invitation, '... since We had resolved to
meet him in person and felt a great longing to converse
with him ...' Alas, in the meantime Strasbourg had definitely
gone over to the Reformation and the letter remained un-
delivered.

The uncertainties of life in Strasbourg are reflected in a
prudent note added to Murner's book by its printer: 'To the
praise and Honour of God Almighty, also in defence of His
Royal Majesty of England, and for the profitableness of all
secular rulers, I, Johann Grieninger, citizen of Strasbourg,
have printed this book in the good hope that nobody will
blame me for having done so, although several people have

approached me and advised me to leave it to another printer
and so forth. Pray, let any charitable man consider well that
I must make my living by handling this as well as any other
printing job. . . .'

Very soon, still in 1523, a curious reply to Murner's book
was published in Germany, *Answer to Murner's Question
whether the King of England be a Liar, or the divine Doctor
M. Luther.*[55] The author's identity remains undiscovered and
his effort is excessively poor; intoxicated by his own almost
unbelievably mighty and bombastic eloquence, the writer,
it seems, never came to the point at all.

In 1524 Murner was at work, printing on a private press a
further book in defence of the King's cause, with the intention of dedicating it to Henry VIII, when a mob raided his
lodgings. Of all the losses suffered on this occasion, Murner
felt most keenly the disappearance of this unfinished work.
Repeatedly he wrote to the town councillors, urging them to
assist towards its recovery; six years later, on May 19th, 1530,
he seemed still unconsoled about the loss and claimed 200
guilders as compensation. Nothing more was known of this
project until in 1930 a chance discovery was made in the University Library of Munich. A beautifully printed but incom-
plete book was found, entitled *Mendatia Lutheri in Serenis-
simum Anglorum et Fratiae Regem Henricum Octavum.* Having made the discovery, Dr. Paul Scherrer soon identified the
fragment as the beginning of a Latin version of Murner's
German book *Whether the King of England or Luther be a
Liar.*[56] Beyond any doubt this is Murner's book as far as it had
progressed at the time when his house was looted. The book
begins as a straight translation of the former German version,
but later on there are considerable variants.

12

Luther did not trouble himself to write an answer to Bishop
Fisher's and Sir Thomas More's refutations of his reply to
Henry VIII. The King now turned his attention elsewhere
and renewed his efforts to rouse the German princes against
Luther, pointing out to them that it would be below his

dignity to quarrel with so despicable a person. One can be quite certain that at this time he seriously regarded himself as the defender of the Church, and one can presume that the contrast between the prolific flattery he was accustomed to hear about his competence as a theologian and the lack of respect shown by Luther offended his vanity.

It was not the first time that the King had addressed himself to German princes regarding the Lutheran affairs. In May 1521, before the publication of his book, he had tried to rouse Ludwig, the Palatine Elector, against the reformer:

'It is not alone on your account, but even more on account of the Holy Christian Faith, that we deplore that fire which Luther has kindled in German lands and which he has kept burning by develish crafts.... What more shameful, dishonest and despicable thing could have happened to the German nation than that in its midst a man should grow up and rise, who, more in frivolity and arrogance of his bad and evil mind than from any, even the smallest, consideration for the honour and entity of Christian doctrine ... dares to interpret the divine laws, the sentences and statutes of the holy fathers and the time-honoured decretals.... [The Elector should therefore] quickly and speedily put hands to the extinction of this poisonous, infectious and inheritable pestilence, in order to prevent certain ruin in the very near future....'[57]

At this point, in 1523, Henry sent Edward Lee to the Archduke Ferdinand, admitting him to the order of the Garter and urging him to take action against Luther. In his oration to Ferdinand, Lee said that 'nothing could be more acceptable to the King (who as well with his sword as with his pen has always endeavoured himself to the tuition and defence of the Christian Faith) than to hear and understand that his good cousin and nephew shall persist in this godly and meritorious purpose'.[58]

Henry also sent an envoy with identical letters to the princes of Saxony, to the Elector Frederick and his brother John, and to Duke George. Recalling to them the ancient bonds of blood relationship, the King asked them for concerted action. Apparently he was under the mistaken impression that Duke George also had jurisdiction over Wittenberg.

The King's envoy went first to Nuremberg, where the Imperial Diet was assembled, and there contacted Hans von der Planitz, the Elector Frederick's ambassador to the Diet. On April 13th Planitz reported to his prince: 'To-day an English herald visited me and asked me for information as to where he could find your grace', adding that the herald had told him that he had a letter to convey: 'I presume', Planitz continued, 'it refers to the Lutheran cause; I will give your grace further information if I can at all find out what the letter contains.'

From the first meeting in Nuremberg, Henry's envoy had made it known that he also intended to visit Duke George, Luther's most determined opponent among the princes. As neither Planitz nor the Elector could have known that this arrangement was based on a misunderstanding on Henry VIII's part, they were at first somewhat apprehensive about the mission of the King's herald. Planitz therefore did what he could to make Henry's man talk about his business, but three days later he still could not report any progress: 'He is very cautious in conversation particularly as far as Luther is concerned, and will not open up. I have made arrangements for people to visit him and to eat with him and to talk to him about all sorts of things, but he would not shoot it off (*hatt aber nicht losschissen wollen*).'

However, a few days later, on April 24th, Planitz knew a little more: 'I have tried my very best (unobtrusively though, as if I knew all about it) to find out from him about what matter he had been sent. Until recently, I have not been able to get much out of him but yesterday he began, quite of his own accord, to relate to me, among other things, that his King has given him orders to convey good news to your Grace as to a friend, and that the King recommends himself most friendly to your Grace. Secondly he said, he had a jewel to present to your Grace and that your Grace will be invited to accept it as a favour. Thirdly he has some letters to hand over and he will await a friendly reply. This, he said, is his mission and nothing more. He also would be willing to give answer to any questions he might be asked. To-day he remarked he would not feel comfortable before arriving at his destination, being received by your Grace and obtaining a favourable answer. He was also asked whether the King is offended about the book which Luther wrote against him; he answered that in England nobody talked about it, that the thing is totally ignored over there. . . . He is full of praise for the House of Saxony and says the King of England derived from the same race and from the Dukes of Saxony. He is full of friendly words but I cannot tell whether he really means them seriously. The herald knows French, English (because he comes from England), Lombardic, Italian but not by any means perfectly. He often mixes his languages. Dutch and German he knows too, but not well, and no Latin.

'I intend to depart with him to Grimma to-morrow, Saturday, where I will detain him for a day's rest so that he shall not arrive before your Grace knows something . . .' After dealing with some other matters, Planitz added a postscript to his letter: 'Also I notice that he speaks French quite well; I suppose he will make his address to your Grace in the French tongue.'[59]

Two days later, the English envoy relieved everybody's anxiety about the contents of the letter addressed to Duke George by telling somebody that all his letters were identical. Frederick was now urging Planitz to speed up the progress to Colditz, but there was some further delay as Planitz's horses were ill and the party had to make use exclusively of the English envoy's three horses; consequently they had to travel by carriage.[60]

On April 28th the Elector wrote to his brother, Duke John, about the visit of Henry's envoy: '. . . Firstly he submitted a message of friendly greetings in accordance with the general custom and so forth, then he handed over a letter which is addressed to you, to my cousin George and to myself. Further he presented me with a book which the King is said to have written himself; it is the book as you may know, issued against Doctor Martinus. There is a note in the book saying that the Pope has issued some indulgences for those who read it and at the end of the book the letter addressed to us is printed word by word, just like the one of which I send you herewith a German translation, precisely the same letter which the herald has delivered to me. . . . I can't tell you anything more. To-morrow he will ride off to my cousin.' The letter ends with Frederick's request for John's opinion on the matter.[61]

The replies given to Henry VIII's envoy were of little use

to the King. Frederick and John wrote a pious epistle, well
stocked with scriptural references, explaining that in their
opinion the Lutheran affair could only be judged competently
by a general council of the Church and certainly not by secular princes. One can hardly expect that Henry VIII had any
patience with such an opinion since he considered his own
competence in such matters quite adequate. And Duke
George, permanently afflicted with an impotent rage as far as
Luther was concerned, was in no need of special admonitions
from England. His only trouble was that, apart from complaining abundantly, he was unable to do anything because
Wittenberg lay outside his territory. At least the bitter
opinions expressed in Duke George's reply were satisfactory
since they echoed Henry's own sentiments, and the King
caused his reply to be printed in England soon afterwards.
Needless to say, the reply of Frederick and John was not considered fit for publication and was simply ignored.[62]

Comparing the two reactions, one would surely tend to expect that the King's envoy might have enjoyed a far warmer
reception with Duke George than with the Elector. Strangely
enough, the reverse was the case. The herald was infuriated
with the want of civility accorded to him by Duke George.
After his departure from Saxony, the Elector's secretary Spalatinus reported to his prince:

'Mulman tells me that the English herald was deeply
offended because Duke George kept him waiting so very
long. I have been told that all the time he praised your Grace
as a noble prince and that he said, your Grace were a much
better prince, a German prince, nay an Elector, and that you
had dealt with him graciously and princely.

'Of the golden and silver coins presented to him by your
Grace he said, he would keep them throughout his life and
bequeath them to the church thereafter. He is deeply offended
that Duke George did not receive him at all . . . he remained
at an inn for the whole time and conversed with Mulman and
Gabriel about wars and such things. Nobody from the castle
honoured him in any way, except that his expenses were seen
to. He never had any guests; neither did he want any, with
the one exception of a compatriot of his who came once to
have supper with him; Mulman thinks this was a priest born

in his own town of Calais whom the castellan had met in the market of Leipzig. But Mulman said that, to judge by his Latin, he did not appear to be so great a scholar as he is reputed to be.

'Thomas von der Heide, one of Duke George's secretaries, came to dine with him once or twice. On one occasion, this secretary was ordered to tell him he should revel and feast and have a good time until his business would be seen to. He then said to Gabriel and Mulman: "What! Having a good time and revelling! I am here not for the sake of eating and frying apples! I am here to look after the affairs of my lord king!" He was rather bored and constantly praised your Electoral Grace . . . and said: "Oh, the pious—oh, the wise Elector of Saxony!"

'At long last, Dr. Kuchler and the Commandant of Leipzig gave him reply last Monday, at a very late hour. Dr. Kuchler presided and made him a present, after the surrender of Duke George's reply, of thirty-five silver guilders, as a gift of honour. The herald complained about the gift and said to Mulman, he thought the prince had given more and that half of it had gone into somebody else's pocket.

'He also said: "Look at that Commandant! What a man he is! He never touched his biretta to me! He never really looked at me, although I am not here for myself and in my own affairs but for my King. What a different man is the Elector of Saxony! He knows how to receive people. As soon as I addressed his Electoral Grace he took off his biretta"—and likewise, he said, your Grace's brother. . . .

'. . . The servant of the herald, a Fleming, praises your Electoral Grace as much as does his lord and is reported to have said: "The pious prince! Throughout my whole life I will never forget him. As long as I live I will pray for him. I would not mind serving him all my life."

'Mulman thinks, the herald should be in Erfurt to-day.

'Your Grace's obedient servant
'Spalatinus.'

Part II

LUTHER'S APOLOGY OF 1525 AND ITS RECEPTION BY HENRY VIII

THE determined attempts of Christian II of Denmark to revive the union of Scandinavian countries, which had been established in 1397 at Kalmar, could not fail to be regarded as a threat to the influence of the Hanse, particularly of Lübeck, in the north. A rebellion broke out, instigated from Lübeck, against the King of Sweden and in Denmark. In 1523 Christian was compelled to leave his country and to apply for assistance to his brother-in-law, Charles V. Before his deposition he had been in touch with Luther, and Carlstadt had been invited to Denmark. The wish of this king to promote a Lutheran reformation in his realm, however, seemed due less to religious considerations than to his hostility towards the bishops and to his appetite for the possessions of the Church. The Reformation, strictly speaking, began in Denmark when Friedrich von Holsten-Gottorp, as Christian's successor, granted toleration to Protestantism, thus enabling Hans Tausen to achieve rapid results in his reformation activities. Christian II himself reverted to Catholicism in 1531 in order to gain allies and assistance for an expedition to the north. He died a prisoner of his own former subjects in 1544.[63]

Some time during the year 1525, this exiled king wrote a letter either to the Elector Frederick or to Spalatinus—he knew Luther and his circle personally, having lived at Wittenberg for a time during the beginning of his exile—to pass to the Lutherans the information that Henry VIII of England had come to be 'inclined towards the Gospel'. He suggested that Luther should approach the English King with an apology which would be received most graciously. Now, Spalatinus had been among those of Luther's friends who had taken a critical view of Luther's rude reply to Henry VIII's

E

book. It was he who told the news to Luther. The latter
was quite sceptical of Henry VIII's alleged change of con-
victions, but Spalatinus managed to persuade him to write
out a sketch for a conciliatory letter. Luther sent the draft to
Spalatinus, 'to give you an opportunity of seeing it so that
you can indicate to me whether anything should be added or
altered'. Spalatinus returned the draft with the comment
that the letter ought to be written in a far more submissive
manner. Luther replied, he would try to comply: 'I will pray
as much as I can (*orabo quoque quantum posse*) and write it
in due course. Just at present there is no time.'

The result of Luther's labours was a lengthy letter to Henry
VIII, written on September 1st, 1525, in which he apologized
for his rude book so meekly and submissively that a German
biographer remarked aptly that but for his monastic background and training, Luther could never have achieved its
composition. In fact Luther wrote under a double misappre-
hension: not only was there no foundation for Christian II's
remarks about Henry VIII's inclination towards the Reformation, but Luther had in the meantime heard another rumour
which anticipated events by two years—that Cardinal Wolsey
had fallen from grace. Much of Luther's apology to the King
is based on this presumption; the letter strongly suggests that
Wolsey was the instigator of all past troubles.

'Grace and Peace in Christ Jesus, our Lord and Saviour,
Amen.

'Illustrious King and Prince!

'Shame should prevent me from writing to Your Royal
Highness and Majesty, since I know so well that I have given
offence to Your Royal Highness with the book against Your
Majesty, the hasty and speedy printing of which was neces-
sitated not through me but through those who are not well
disposed towards Your Majesty. However, I draw confidence
and courage through Your Majesty's natural graciousness of
which many people have told me in letters and by word of
mouth, day by day and evermore frequently. And therefore
I presume that Your Royal Highness, in the awareness of
being mortal, will not countenance eternal wrath and
hostility.

'Furthermore, I have been told by trustworthy people that

the book which was published under the dignified name of
the King of England was not in fact Your Majesty's own, as
was broadcast by the cunning sophists who thus misused
Your Majesty's title and name. They did not realize what
peril they would bring upon themselves by heaping shame
and dishonour upon the Royal Name, especially and above
all others that monstrous beast, hated by God and by men,
the Cardinal of Eborac, that pernicious plague and desola-
tion of Your Majesty's kingdom. That is why it came to pass
that now I am so ashamed that I dare not lift up my eyes
to Your Majesty, to so exalted a potentate and mighty a king,
considering that I am quite unworthy, a despised person, a
mere worm, who should have been rendered helpless simply
by means of contempt, as being unworthy of any attention.

'Now, however low and contemptible I may be, yet have I
been moved to write to Your Majesty because I have heard
the news that Your Majesty is well inclined towards the Gospel and bears great displeasure towards those dissolute,
damnable people. My heart has received such reports as a
veritable gospel, that is to say as good tidings.

'Therefore I prostrate myself with this letter before the feet
of Your Majesty and I pray and implore Your Majesty for
gracious forgiveness and pardon for everything wherewith I
have given offence to Your Majesty. With the greatest
humility granted to me, I ask for the sake of Christ's passion
and for His Honour, as Christ Himself has prayed and asked
us to forgive, one to the other, all sin and mistakes.

'Further, if it is not contrary to Your Majesty's desire, I
would offer to Your Majesty a recantation and I would render
honour to Your Majesty by the means of a printed book. I
pray to be graciously informed of your wish and I would do
it willingly and without delay. Although compared with Your
Majesty I can only be regarded as a despicable person of no
importance, much common good and the promotion of the
Gospel and of God's honour could be hoped for if I were permitted to address Your Royal Grace of England in the matter
relating to the Gospel.

'Meanwhile I pray that God, who has begun it, will cause
Your Majesty to grow and increase in the attainment of the
inclination and the obedience towards the Gospel with your
whole spirit and that poisonous mouths will neither fill

your ears nor conquer your heart; those flatterers and
sweet-spoken hypocrites cannot help declaring that Luther is a
heretic. It would be better if Your Majesty were to consider
it independently, as follows: what can possibly be evil in
Luther's teaching, considering he teaches nothing else but
that we shall be redeemed by faith in Jesus Christ, the Son
of God, who suffered for us, died and rose again as it is clearly
witnessed in the Holy Gospels and in the writings of the
apostles. For this is the main article, the firm ground of my
teaching on which I continue building and teaching: of
charity towards one's neighbour, of obedience to secular
authority and mortification of the sinful flesh, as is asked from
us in our Christian doctrine.

'What, then, is wrong or evil in these main articles of my
teaching? Let people wait and listen before they pronounce
judgment. Why am I being condemned without being heard
and overcome?

'I also chastise the abuse and tyranny of the bishops who
teach differently (nay, the very opposite) from the main
article mentioned above; who chase after tithes, rents, splen-
dour, lust of the flesh, yea after kingdoms, empires and who
want to seize all the world's riches for themselves. Do not
even the common people know this and condemn it? And
they themselves must admit that it is true. Why do they not
improve themselves and provide sound teaching if they wish
to remain unhated and unpunished?

'No doubt, Your Majesty is well informed which great
princes in Germany, which communities, towns and many
greatly learned men make common cause with me and, God
be thanked, will not suffer to see me condemned. I pray that
God, our Lord, will also add Your Majesty to their number
and put you apart from the murderers of souls.

'Why should one be astonished that the Emperor and
various princes rail and rage against me? Do we not read in
the second Psalm: "Why do the heathen rage and the people
imagine a vain thing? The kings of the earth set themselves
and the rulers take council together against the Lord and his
anointed"? On the contrary, it is miraculous if a single king
or prince becomes fond of the Gospel. Oh, how I desire with
all my power that I should rejoice and jubilate about such a
miracle were it wrought with Your Majesty too. And the Lord

for whose eyes and by whose will I am writing this, may lend strength and power to my words so that the King of England may soon become a perfect disciple of the Lord Jesus Christ and, in addition, Luther's gracious lord, Amen.

'If it pleases Your Majesty, I await a gracious and kind answer. Given at Wittenberg on the 1st of September, Anno 1525.

Your Majesty's obedient servant
D. Martin Luther.'

There cannot be any doubt that the element of submissive apology in Luther's letter can only be read in the light of a presumption that Henry VIII might have begun to reconsider his attitude towards the Lutherans' own reformation. The cringing tone of the opening of Luther's letter should not divert the reader's attention from the all-important fact that the letter is an *offer of apology* rather than a definite apology, an offer strictly dependent on a verification of the King's alleged change of mind.

Henry replied after a long delay which he excused by writing that he had been travelling throughout his realm for a long while, and that Luther's letter had therefore taken some time to reach him. His answer was aggressively ungracious and most vigorously dispelled any such expectations as those cherished by Christian II of Denmark.

Once again, it is impossible to say with any certainty who actually wrote the reply, whether it was the King himself, Vives[64] or someone else. It was certainly written immediately after the King had seen Luther's letter. Henry desired to make his reply known as quickly as possible among the German princes, together with a copy of Luther's letter. There was some delay, however, owing to the fact that at the crucial moment Luther's letter could not be found; it was only known that it had last been in the possession of Sir Thomas More.[65] The King became impatient, but Wolsey strongly advised against the dispatch of his reply without the text of Luther's letter. Some time in September 1526 he wrote to Sir Thomas More:

'Where as you haue notified vnto me, that the Kingis pleasor is, that his Gracis aunswer to Luthers lettre shold be immedietly sent forth to the princes of Almayne, without

abiding or tarying for the copy therof, I thinke therin that
meseemeth it is not convenient that this shuld be doon, in my
poore opinion; aswel for that Luther, who is ful of sutelte
and craft, herafter might percase denye that any such lettre
hath been sent by hym vnto the Kingis Highnes, as that the
said answer, not having the said copy adioyned therunto,
shuld be, for want therof, to the reders and herers therof,
sumwhat diminute and obscure and not perfitely perceyved
by them that shal rede the same.'[66]

The King's reply was first printed in a magnificent presentation edition for illustrious readers; the initials were not
printed but inserted by an artistic hand. The ordinary edition
was printed a little later by Pynson. In 1528 an English version of the new dispute was published under the title *A copy
of the lettres wherin the most redoubted and mighty Prince
our souerayne lorde kynge Henry the eighth ... made
answere vnto a certayne letter of Martyn Luther* ... It is from
this edition that the following extracts are quoted. The book
opens with a long introduction in which the King addresses
his subjects.

'Martyn Luther late a frere Augustyn and now ron out i
apostasy and wedded hath nat onely scraped owt of the
asshen and kyndeled agayne almost all the embres of those
foule errours and heresyes that euer heretyke helde sythe
Christ was borne hytherto; but hath also added some so poy-
soned pointes of his owne so wretched, so vyle, so detestable,
provokynge men to myschefe, encoragyng the worlde to syn
... that neuer was there erst any heretyke so farre voyde of
all grace and wyt, that durst for shame speke them. ...'

In a modest tone he recalls how, years ago, 'entendyng for
our parte somwhat to set hande therto, wrote after our meane
lernyng a lytell tretyse ...' and goes on to say that, by now,
Luther is forsaken by all and in despair. 'Wyse men espye
hym, lerned men leaue hym, good men abhorre hym.'
As to Luther's letter, the King advised his subjects: 'By
the sight wherof ye may partely parceyue bothe what the
man is in hym selfe and of what sorte is his doctryne: whiche
two thinges if ye well pondre ye shall soone vnderstande his
doctryne so abhominable that it must nedes make the man

odious and shewe hym to be naught were hys lyueng in
apperence neuer so good and the man hym selfe of lyueng so
openly naught & vycious that hys open vyces and boldely
bosted wretchednesse must nedes make his doctryne suspected.'

There follow some special admonitions against heretical
trends. Particularly, the people should not 'truste to moche
youre owne commentes and interpretatyons but in euery
doute that shall insourge lerne the truthe and encyclue to the
same by the aduice of your pastorall fathers of the soule. . . .'

In his reply to Luther, the King begins with a summary of
the latter's communication. 'These be Luther all thynges
whiche were in your letter contayned: in whiche, as we right
well perceyve your couvert fraudulent purpose so shal we
on the othersyde after our accustome plynesse (lest your craft
wayes might abuse gode simple folke) to euery poynt gyue
you trewe and open answere.'

The King offered severe criticism of Luther's marriage with
Katharina von Bora: 'ye beyng a Frere haue taken a Nonne:
& not onely vyolate her (whiche if ye had done among the
olde Romayns that were paynyns she shulde haue been buried
quicke and ye beaten to deth) but also which mouche worse
is haue openly maried her & by that menes openly abused
her in synne. . . .'

Henry made his attitude to Luther's reforming activities
very plain: '. . . what ruynous buylding ye reare upon the false
foundation of your unfaythfull faythe. . . . Ye were iustly
condempned seying that ye were condempned by our holy
father the pope and the holy college of cardynals: whose
iustyce and indifference there wyll no wyse man any thynge
mistrust. . . . Surely there was neuer man borne (I trowe)
that set so moche by hymselfe that has so lytell cause. . . .'

There is a memorable passage in which Henry VIII particularly attacked those aspects of the Lutheran reforms
which resulted in monks and nuns leaving their communities:
'. . . good religious folke be dayly by your meanes expelled
oute of their places in whiche they were determyned in
chastity, prayer and fastynge to bestow their lyves i goddess
seruice. . . .'

Luther's remarks about Wolsey produced a warm eulogy
from the King: 'Your pestilent tong is so leude to rayle vpon

the most reuerende father in god, the lorde legate Cardynall of yorke, oure chefe counsailour & Chaunceller, it greueth hym lytell (I wot well) to be rayled vpon, with your blasphemous tong that rayleth and rageth against christes hole churche, his saints, his apostles, his holy mother and hym selfe as it euidently (as well by many partes of your pestylent bokes as by the furious acts of your faction) appereth. And his fatherhode nowe is and shalbe so moche in more cordyall fauoure with me ... his fatherhode is in this one poynt to my realme very gode and holsome in that he conformable to my mynde and accordyng to my comaundement studously pourgeth my realm from the pestylent contagion of your factious heresyes.'

Finally, the King informed Luther that no further disputation with him was intended: 'I am long syns at a poynt no more to vouchsafe to dyspute any mar with you sith I have had good experience of you howe clene ye set all reason asyde and fall to raylinge. For which I have determyned (which I shal surely keepe) as for any dispytions to leave you to your lewdnesse ... But as for me I well knowe and knowledge that I am unable of my selfe to the understanding thereof (i.e. the Gospel) and therefore callyng for godd's helpe most humbly submitte my selfe to the determynation of Christes Church and interpretations of the olde holy fathers. ...'

In the course of the King's reply to Luther, the doctrine of justification by faith is rejected and Luther's denial of free will criticized. Of course, the King did not forget to make Luther responsible for the Peasants' War.

Since Luther had no intention of writing a reply to Henry VIII's answer, this might have been the end of the matter. Henry had certainly interpreted Luther's letter correctly in recognizing that Luther would never recant. Henry had no knowledge of the intervention of Christian II which had been the cause of Luther's letter; neither could he have guessed that Luther had been most reluctant, and had only written at the urgent request of his friends. The King was simply of the opinion that Luther was desperate and was trying to find new supporters.

In Germany, too, Luther's opponents made the most of the supposition that he was casting around for new allies, and declared, whether through careless reading or from the desire to exploit to the fullest extent any new happening, that Luther had offered a recantation if thereby he could win over Henry VIII to his faction.

Henry VIII's reply was reprinted in Cologne with a preface by Cochlaeus in which Luther's offer of a recantation was alleged. Hieronymus Emser reprinted Luther's letter to the King of England under the title *Epistola M. Lutheri ad Henricum VIII Angliae ac Franciae Regem etc in qua veniam petit eorum que prius stultus ac precepin eundem regem affuderit: offeres palinodiam se cantarum.* . . . Emser also published a German translation of Luther's letter, and here again he made mention of Luther's offer to recant. The procedure was, once again, typical of the fashion in which controversies were conducted and prolonged in the sixteenth century; although Luther's letter, made available to his readers by Emser, contained no such offer, Emser felt entitled to pretend to scoring a point, however ineffectually in the end, against his opponent. To his German translation Emser added a dedicatory preface addressed to Margareta, Princess of Anhalt, in which he provided a most sensational if totally imaginary picture of ecclesiastical life among the Lutherans: 'In one place, women sing the Mass, in another shoemakers do the preaching; at best all their preachers are either runaway monks or anthematized clerks who stand in the pulpits in secular habit, with cut trousers and shoes, spewing fire, clamour for the abandonment of secular government and authority and rail towards heaven. If the poor blind people had but a single drop of understanding, they would see quickly that it is plainly a devilish and false thing, committed by Luther. . . .'

After having demonstrated that Luther had failed miserably in all his enterprises, Emser wrote: 'since God was against him, he now meekly and hypocritically creeps to the kings and princes which before he had openly offended, secretly praying for pardon, and has the audacity to attract them to his gospel by the means of his false flattery'.

Luther had long since decided not to answer any more of Emser's writings whatever they might contain. However, Emser's news of his alleged offer of recantation was broadcast with such insistence that he had to make a declaration of the true position. He wrote a booklet *Against the Title of the English King's slanderous Writing.* . . .[67] This was not meant to be a reply to Henry VIII's answer but simply a defence against the *title* under which the King's reply had been published in Germany. Emser promptly wrote a further booklet in which he admitted that he had formulated the title; with the customary verbosity, he carried out a syllogistical defence against Luther's complaint that he had deliberately broadcast a lie and wrote lengthy explanations of the meaning of the crucial words in the title: *offeres palinodiam se cantarum.* Luther left Emser's defence unanswered.

The alleged offer of a recantation was repeated in print by others such as, for instance, Cochlaeus and John Faber in 1528. The former mentioned it, referring to Luther's 'secret and sealed' letter to Henry VIII, in the preface to his translation of the Bishop of Rochester's writings against Oecolompadius.[68] In the preface he also extolled the merits of all English efforts against Luther, especially those of 'the most mighty King who on our behalf has taken the trouble to write and dispute on our side in aid of God's cause (unprecedented considering he is a king, and therefore truly marvellous)'. John Faber visited England in 1528 as an ambassador of Archduke Ferdinand. Immediately after this journey he published an *Instruction and Answer of Doctor Johann Fabri relating to Martin Luther's angry and detestable writing containing his offer of recantation given to his Grace, the King of England.*[69] Faber, incidentally, is full of praise for Henry VIII's learning: 'I will tell you for sure,' he writes in the book, addressing Luther, 'the King of England has conversed with me for a while in such excellent Latin that I was truly astonished.'

This is a convenient point to mention the many books dedicated to English dignitaries by German opponents of Luther as a demonstration of their gratitude. Such dedications became very frequent after 1525. Eck dedicated most editions of his *Enchiridion locorum communium adversus Lutheranos* to Henry VIII, one of which includes a letter addressed to Sir Thomas More. Cochlaeus dedicated most of his output of the years 1525–29 to Englishmen.[70] In his list of dedications the King's name appears only on one occasion; Cochlaeus was deeply disappointed and offended because Henry VIII never favoured him with a letter or a present in return for his interruption of Tyndale's printing activities in Cologne; only

Bishops Fisher, Ridley and West sent him letters and presents.

In England, the second stage in the controversy between Henry VIII and Luther was followed by a renewed and determined effort to stamp out Lutheran influences.

In his reply to Luther, the King had stated in no uncertain terms that Luther was quite wrong in presuming that the *Assertio Septem Sacramentorum* had been written or instigated by Cardinal Wolsey or that the King had since regretted the publication of the book. A few years later, Henry VIII was to accuse Sir Thomas More of such an instigation: '. . . by his subtill synister sleyghtes, [he] most vnnaturallie procuring and provokye him to set forth a booke of the Assertion of the seven sacramentes and maintaynaunce of the Popes aucthorytie, had caused him, to his dishonour throughoute all Christendome, to put a sword in to the Popes handes to fight against him selfe. . . .' More then replied: '. . . My lordes, these terrours be argumentes for children, and not for me. But to answere that wherewith you doe chifly birden me, I beleave the kinges highnes of his honour will neuer lay that to my charge; for none is there that can in that pointe say in my excuse more than his highnes himself, who right well knoweth that I neuer was procurer nor concelour of his maiestye thereunto; but after it was finished, by his graces appojntment and consent of the makers of the same, only a sorter out and placer of the principall matters therin contayned.'[71]

In 1534 this was Henry VIII's attitude towards his own book and towards the finest man among his subordinates. Only thirteen years had passed since Cardinal Wolsey had written to him: 'I suppose noon of your subgiettes, of whatever state and condicion they bee, knoweth better the integritie of your vertuous mynde, in the faithfull observaunces of your oothe, faithe, and promises, wherin surely, and without adulation, fewe Princes may be compared; for if all other princes were as constant and scrupulous in keping their oothes, faithe, promise as ye bee, not oonely amities shulde remaigne inviolate [and] unbroken, but also restfull tranquillitie and peax established in Christendom.'

Part III

THE DIVORCE AND WITTENBERG

A FULL account of Henry VIII's attempts to obtain a declaration of nullity in respect of his marriage with Catherine of Aragon would go beyond the intentions of this book. However, a summary of the most important stages of the involved affair must be given for three reasons. Firstly, the part which the Wittenberg theologians were invited to play must be shown in the context of all other schemes. Secondly, the very fact that Henry VIII appealed to Luther for a favourable verdict is linked with that aspect of the divorce episode which was to have the most consequences in English history. Finally, the unattractive story of the divorce is, without doubt, the cause of the Henrican reformation, and therefore not only the missions to Wittenberg but the whole affair has remained 'controversial', largely through the good offices of historians who regard it as their moral duty to ignore (or, alas, to 'interpret') whatever, in their judgment, is too bad to be true.

Here, then, is a brief summary of Henry's problem and of the methods he chose for its solution. In 1503 Henry VII had applied to Pope Julius II for a dispensation permitting his second son—the future Henry VIII—to marry Catherine of Aragon, widow of Henry VII's other son Arthur. Such a marriage was so clearly forbidden by Canon Law that, at first, Julius II replied to the effect that he was not sure whether he could possibly grant such a dispensation. Eventually, however, the dispensation was issued, yet not at all to everybody's satisfaction; the legality of the marriage was still debated after the papal decision had taken effect.[72]

On January 31st, 1510, Catherine gave birth to her first child; it was still-born. On January 1st, 1511, a son was born who died after three days. In September 1513 another son was either still-born or died immediately after birth. In June 1514 yet another son died as soon as he was born. Several further miscarriages followed in later years, but in between, in 1516, a daughter was born who lived, Princess Mary.

As early as 1514, a rumour went around that Henry VIII intended to repudiate his Queen 'because he is unable to have children by her and intends to marry a daughter of the French Duke of Bourbon'.[73] It appears, however, that there was no foundation for the rumour which was begun by diplomatic gossip.[74] Henry's concern about the prospects of having a son turned to fresh hope after the survival of Mary. There followed many anxious years in which the birth of a son was eagerly but vainly expected; this alone could have brought certainty to the succession.

It seems that it was in the year 1525 that Henry's hope faded and, soon afterwards, it became a matter of primary importance to obtain a separation from Catherine, which would enable him to marry again.

Already at this stage we can summarize the magnitude of the problem which Henry VIII had to face. No such thing as divorce, in the modern secular meaning of the term, is provided by Canon Law. The solution to be aimed at was a declaration to the effect that the King's marriage with Catherine was null and void, that it was not, and had never been, a marriage. In this particular case the 'impediment' chosen by Henry was that the papal dispensation of 1503 had been granted erroneously, and that therefore his cohabitation with Catherine had not been a marriage but an illicit, sinful union. The urgency with which the negotiations were opened was not at all the result, as one reads so frequently, of the spell cast over Henry by Anne Boleyn; this only accelerated the later stages of the affair. The all-important motive was Henry's awareness that only a son of his, born legitimately, could secure the succession. This alone was the reason for Henry's frantic efforts to secure favourable verdicts from outside authorities even at a time when he had already solved the problem and gained complete, even despotic, ecclesiastical power in England. Henry VIII knew quite clearly what was needed. Until January 1531 he pursued this definite aim with unrelenting logic; thereafter, special circumstances began to dictate the course of events. This summary of the King's prob-

Ob der künig vß engelland ein lügner sey oder der Luther.

IV. Thomas Murner's Tract *Whether the King of England or Luther is a Liar* (1523). Title page.

lem and the solution envisaged by him must be kept in mind constantly; otherwise the story of the divorce becomes a succession of dissolute intrigues.

Henry VIII began by declaring that his conscience was troubled by the realization that his marriage was illicit, that he and the Queen had been living in sin for over twenty years. We will not pronounce judgment whether or not the King had a conscience capable of being disturbed or whether his spiritual conflict—if there was one—ought to be interpreted as a superstitious reaction to the Queen's miscarriages. Even if Henry VIII's motives were noble and deeply religious, his methods were, and not only by modern standards, from the very beginning and throughout appalling. They began with a 'shameful device' (J. Gairdner), the staging of a mock trial in which Henry VIII was summoned to defend himself before the papal legate—Cardinal Wolsey!—on the charge of living in sinful cohabitation with the wife of his deceased brother Arthur. The conduct of the trial ended, practically, with the reading of this charge, after which the 'court' adjourned without coming to a decision.

Henry was fully aware that the achievement of his wish was not easy and that the likelihood of overcoming the immense difficulties depended upon a judicious choice of approach. He was sufficiently informed in matters of Canon Law—and in the virtuosity of his epoch in overcoming even its plainest injunctions—to know that it was not impossible to obtain a declaration of nullity if only he could manage to steer clear of political implications, and if he could also somehow make it possible for the Pope to comply without incurring a loss of papal prestige. His first aim was to make arrangements for the case to be tried in England and then to gain the Pope's agreement with the decision arrived at. Such subsidiary difficulties created problem after problem in the course of time. A declaration of nullity would have amounted to an admission on the part of the Pope that a recent predecessor of his had granted a dispensation erroneously. The Pope could hardly be expected to show great eagerness to admit a papal error in an important dispensation, at a time when the judiciary function of the Holy See was more strongly debated in the world than ever before and totally rejected by the Lutherans. Furthermore, Catherine

F

of Aragon was the aunt of the Emperor Charles V, who made it absolutely clear that he would assist her. Even if the Pope may have wished to oblige Henry VIII (who, of course, did not fail to point out that he had good justification for appealing to papal gratitude), he could ill afford to offend the Emperor. The Queen's attitude was determined by a very simple reaction: she had no reason whatever to regard her marriage with a disturbed conscience. The dispensation of 1503 had been regarded as valid for many, many years. Further, although that dispensation had provided for the possibility that her marriage with Prince Arthur might have been consummated, Catherine, solemnly declared that her earlier marriage had *not* been consummated—the most decisive reason for her to regard her marriage with Henry VIII as perfectly legitimate; a declaration of nullity would have implied that she had lived knowingly in an incestuous union, a proposition which she refused to accept. Moreover, her daughter Mary would figure as the issue of a sinful union and her claim to the succession would cease automatically. Henry began the great scheme with his characteristic self-assurance, but soon enough he must have noticed that his determination to obtain the divorce was matched by the Queen's determination to frustrate his attempts.

Henry's plans were already overburdened with a multitude of difficulties before he rendered them quite fantastically involved by his infatuation for Anne Boleyn whom, after having obtained the divorce from Catherine, he was firmly resolved to marry. The peculiar problem here was that Anne Boleyn's sister had been the King's mistress. That is to say, Henry was planning a second marriage which suffered the same impediment as his existing marriage with Catherine. What differences there were hardly suited Henry's arguments in his divorce plans: Catherine's first marriage had not been consummated and her marriage to Henry had been authorized by a special dispensation. How could Henry now pursue the divorce by protesting that, notwithstanding the papal dispensation, a liaison forbidden by Canon Law troubled his conscience?

We have already mentioned the 'trial' in which Henry played the part of the defendant and Wolsey that of the prosecutor. This scheme had to be abandoned when the news of the sack of Rome and Pope Clement's captivity entirely altered the situation. Wolsey in his capacity as papal legate could have conducted the trial and could, as indeed was his intention, have declared the dispensation of 1503 untenable. The *free* Pope *might* have obliged Wolsey and complied with his request to revoke the dispensation, thereby rendering the King's marriage with Catherine null and void; in any case it seemed worth while to make the attempt at a quick solution. But now the Pope was the Emperor's prisoner and it seemed pointless to pursue the scheme.

The Pope's captivity spoiled one chance. But did it not also offer hitherto inconceivable opportunities? Wolsey was not slow to see a new way. He made an arrangement for an assembly of cardinals to meet in France, with himself as the presiding prelate. The idea was to induce the assembly to make a demonstration of loyalty towards the imprisoned Pope—by means of adopting a decision against the interests of the Emperor's aunt! In order to make sure that the Pope, in his plight, would not spoil the game, a loyal motion was proposed that the Pope's authority should be suspended while he was in the Emperor's power. However carefully everything was planned, the cardinals' vote rejected Wolsey's proposition. The second scheme had failed. Wolsey did not give in immediately, but urged Henry to send ambassadors to the Pope demanding his assent to the motion which had failed to find the approval of the cardinals.

From then onwards, Wolsey's activities failed entirely because Henry VIII had not told him he desired to marry Anne Boleyn. Wolsey was still pursuing an older plan whereby Henry was to marry the daughter of Louis XII. Whilst Wolsey worked on one scheme, Henry was busy with another. The King ignored Wolsey's advice to send Ghinucci as an ambassador to the Pope and chose to dispatch his secretary Knight. The mission of this ambassador was totally different from what Wolsey had imagined it to be: he was to obtain the Pope's permission for marrying a second wife, without a divorce from Catherine. When the petition for a solution by means of bigamy was handed again to the Pope in 1528 (by Sir Francis Bryan and Peter Vannes), it had the active support of Wolsey who prepared for the Pope the bull, well

stocked with scriptural references from the Old Testament.
Simultaneously, Knight was to secure a papal dispensation,
similar to that of 1503, enabling Henry to make Anne Boleyn
his second wife despite his earlier association with Anne's
sister. Knight succeeded with this second request: the Pope
granted the dispensation, but only upon the condition that
Henry's marriage with Catherine was first declared null.
Since Henry was not prepared to wait, the dispensation alone
was a fragmentary success which could hardly give him much
satisfaction. Anyway, a week later the Pope was in despair,
actually in tears, when trying to imagine the reaction of the
Emperor should he hear of the dispensation. In actual fact,
Knight's mission had failed.

Equally abortive were all attempts to have the cause tried
in England. At one time the Pope gave his consent. Campeggio was sent to England with a choice of three policies;
he should conduct the trial with Wolsey, or he should persuade Catherine to disappear into a convent, or, as a last
resort, he was to see to it that as much time as possible should
be wasted. In the end, it was the third policy which the
special legate had to adopt. The trial was frustrated by
Catherine who rejected her specially appointed judges and
appealed to Rome. She produced a copy of a brief of Julius II,
the original of which was in the possession of Charles V,
which legitimatized her marriage with Henry beyond any
doubt, even if it had been the case that her first marriage had
been consummated (which she, again, solemnly denied).
Wolsey tried to denounce the brief as a forgery but the Emperor declared that he would be willing to produce the original, but only in Rome.[75]

Catherine also refused quite definitely to go into a convent
unless Henry, too, were to take monastic vows. Now, Henry
was most willing to fulfil this condition, provided he had an
assurance that the Pope would release him from the vows
immediately afterwards while refusing such a release to
Catherine, should she apply. In any case, the most important
point had to be settled first: was it certain that he could marry
again if Catherine took religious vows? It was by no means
certain! The one and only promising aspect of this scheme
was that it would enable the Pope to grant the declaration of
nullity without offending the Emperor, considering that the

Queen had 'deserted' Henry by going into a convent. Campeggio tried hard to make Catherine accept the veil, but she was determined to defend her position.

On June 29th, 1529, the political situation changed once again: suddenly a treaty was made at Barcelona—'indissoluble peace, friendship and treaty'—between the Pope and the Emperor. The Pope promptly announced that Henry's cause could only be heard in Rome, not in England. Henry tried to bribe the Emperor with a gift of 300,000 crowns—in vain. Charles V refused to sell his aunt.

While all this had been going on, the Pope had volunteered his private advice time and again: Henry should go ahead, marry Anne Boleyn, present the Pope with a *fait accompli* and then one would see what could be done.[76] For instance, on January 13th, 1528, Gregory Casale wrote to Wolsey:

'If the king marry again . . . the cause may be examined at Rome, when the Pope will give sentence, and so judgment will be passed to the satisfaction of the whole world, to which neither Spaniard nor German can make objection. This is the method he suggests for proceeding; but he desires it should not be thought to come from himself.'

Of course, Henry's three ambassadors to the Pope at this stage (Casale, Gardiner and Fox) gave the obvious interpretation to this suggestion by calling it 'a device to get rid of responsibility' on the part of the Pope. Henry, however, perceived that Catherine needed only to gain knowledge of such a scheme, write an appeal to Rome and thus forestall Henry's marriage with Anne Boleyn while the case was *sub judice*.[77] We shall return to the Pope's private advice in a different context.

Meanwhile a totally different scheme, suggested by Cranmer and eagerly accepted by the King, had been initiated: in 1528 great and extremely costly efforts were made whereby Henry VIII hoped to gain favourable opinions of his cause from universities. It is quite feasible to regard this as the opening episode of the English Reformation. 'By asking the universities for a verdict, Henry began to question the principle of the Pope's dispensing power.'[78] This opinion of J. Gairdner is borne out by a highly significant conversation between the King and Eustace Chapuys on November 28th, 1529, in which Henry approved of truths which Luther had

brought to light and which he could not reject despite the
reformer's heresy.[79] Approval of Luther, however confined to
certain aspects, in a talk with the newly arrived ambassador
of Charles V was certainly indicative of a new orientation.

The invitation to universities to approve the matrimonial
cause began at Cambridge and Oxford. It took almost half a
year before the King achieved what he wanted. At Oxford
he obtained a favourable verdict very quickly from the
doctors, but the Masters of Arts opposed. Henry informed
them 'how deeply he resented the stubbornness and mis-
behaviour of the Masters of Arts; they seemed to him not to
have lived long enough to qualify them with a capacity and
discretion in this business; that, therefore, they ought to
resign to the judgment of wiser men and be governed by the
precedent of the doctors; that if they held on in their obstin-
acy and gave their sovereign any further trouble, they should
quickly be made sensible of the ill consequence, and understand it was not their best way to provoke a hornet's nest.'[80]
Even after reading this communication, the Masters refused
to alter their verdict. After several further attempts to make
them comply with the royal demand, the Chancellor ordered
the heads to exclude the Masters from the Convocation. This
done, the verdict of the doctors was drawn up formally and
the seal of the university affixed. The Vice-Chancellor then
presented the document to the King who, we are told, was
well pleased.

In the following years, 1529 and 1530, there was enormous
activity in collecting arguments and opinions in favour of the
King's cause.[81] Richard Cooke was sent to Italy to solicit
useful arguments from Italian canonists; handsome rewards
were paid out—sometimes the price was fixed by the supplier
—but it was solemnly asserted that Cooke never bought
opinions. Cooke was not supposed to explain his business. In
order to gain access to some documents in Rome, he posed
as a penitent priest. At another time he adopted the name of
Johannes Flandrensis and pretended to be engaged in investigations relating to a patrimonial affair and private business
of his own and of his brothers. He consulted books and documents and busied himself with wild searches in the writings
of the fathers. He had conferences with Jews about the levitical marriage law.[82]

Cooke did his best to give good service, but Henry did not, of course, just sit back and wait for results; without enlightening Cooke, the King pursued new ideas, some of which imperilled Cooke's activities. In one of his letters complaining about Henry's impatience, Cooke wrote—on August 24th, 1530—that he 'waxed extremely pale' when he was shown a letter of Henry's addressed to the Bishop of Verona.[83]

Italian, French and Dutch universities were invited to state their opinions. Most of them, twelve in all, gave favourable answers which were printed in the form of extracts in 1532. As might be expected, the negative verdict received from the university of Louvain remained unmentioned.

Henry hoped that through these investigations into the opinion of the universities a way might be found to force a decision from the Pope without having the cause tried at Rome. Gradually, however, the incoming results from all these inquiries and researches led to a new approach. Henry VIII had always considered himself as something of an authority in theology and Canon Law and now, having studied or at least perused whatever was found to speak in favour of his desire, his esteem of his own learning was greater than ever before. Unwittingly the Pope gave Henry the cue for asserting his competence: in his anxiety to delay all progress of the King's cause, the Pope had repeatedly declared that it touched on some points of Canon Law of so intricate a quality that he, lacking such detailed knowledge, found himself unable to give definite answers *ex tempore*, that the legal position had to be ascertained most carefully, and so forth. Henry was not slow to react with the proclamation that the Pope's self-confessed ignorance was precisely the reason why the cause should not be examined in Rome but elsewhere; what would be the point of submitting it to the Pope's judgment if the Pope was ignorant? Charles V was informed:

'A judge competent to decide such an affair should be well versed in divine law, as well as that of the Canons, in which the Pope has confessed himself ignorant, as appears both by divers letters addressed by himself to the King and by the reports of the King's ambassadors. How then could the King, without offence to God, having a clear conviction of his own right, submit to the determination of one who acknowledges himself to be ignorant of his science? It would be . . . like putting himself under a blind guide. . . . He does not see what judgment is needed to delay the case any longer, considering that the scripture says *Ubi Spiritus Domini, ibi libertas.* . . . It is clear, therefore, that he is not bound to wait any longer for the decision of the Church. . . .'[84]

Statements of this kind tend to give the impression of a total reorientation on the part of Henry VIII towards the Pope, and by implication, to the Church. Nothing is more misleading than such impressions; the evolution of Henry's reformation was not determined by a profound change of conviction but by momentary expediency. Many of those ideas which had a superficial family likeness to Protestant thought were originally practical experiments, if not simply bluff. It was not entirely due to Henry that most of the bluff actually served to expose the weakness of the Pope and, again, by implication that of the papacy. Had the bluff been able to frighten the Pope into a decision in Henry's favour, Henry would probably have immediately stopped shouting sectarian sentiments. The awareness of scriptural, evangelical 'perfect freedom' was nothing but the by-product of the much more pressing aim to have the papal dispensation of 1503 revoked. It is therefore hardly astonishing that Henry's first utterance of 'protestant' reasoning did not prevent his continuing negotiations with the harassed Pope. On July 10th, 1531, Henry informed his ambassadors Ghinucci, Benet and Casale: 'We do not altogether despair of the pope . . . not that we would ask anything from him, but that he may see the truth and come to his senses.'[85]

A perusal of the reports of Henry's envoys shows that the Pope would have liked nothing better than to see the end of the delicate affair which wasted so much of his time. But he could not force results without doing irreparable damage to his own interests. And thus he was, even more than Henry, reduced to improvising: one day giving secret, private advice to the King to present him with a *fait accompli*, the next day refusing to utter a word, sometimes 'fuming' when exasperated beyond endurance by the tactlessly persistent ambassadors.

There were also times when the Pope tested his own

strength, but this only made Henry realize more clearly that the never-ending uncertainty about his chances with the Pope might well lead to the least welcome kind of certainty. On March 7th, 1530, a papal bull was affixed to the church doors at Bruges, Tournay and Dunkirk denouncing Henry's plan to marry Anne Boleyn. Later in the same month a formal papal proclamation followed, forbidding ecclesiastical doctors, judges, advocates and all the clergy to make pronouncements against Henry's marriage with Catherine. All this gives the superficial impression of finality on the part of the Pope. Actually, it was during the same year that the Pope wished more strongly than ever that Henry would take the step which he had already recommended in 1528—that he should simply marry Anne Boleyn and ask for a confirmation from Rome *post festum*; 'if the marriage took place *bona fide*, the Pope could still legitimatize children of the second marriage, because the marriage had been contracted *bona fides*'.[86] In March 1530—the same month in which he so strongly asserted his prerogative—the Pope told the Bishop of Tarbes that he would be happy if only the second marriage were already contracted, provided it were not interpreted as having been done by his authority, or as indicating a limitation of his power to give dispensations from divine laws.[87] Again, in September 1530, Henry's ambassador Ghinucci reported that the Pope had said in a private conversation that he would with less scandal give the King a dispensation for having two wives; Ghinucci then turned the conversation again to Henry's plan but the Pope came back to the bigamy solution, although he foresaw certain difficulties, especially the fact that the Emperor would never consent to it.[88]

2

Here it is necessary to interrupt the story and to discuss briefly the Pope's preference for bigamy. We shall see later on that Luther also was of the opinion that, compared with divorce, bigamy was the lesser scandal.

There is a curious tendency among some English historians, by no means confined to Roman Catholics, not only to

preserve a conspiratorial silence about the Pope's genuine conviction but to follow up their silence about the Pope with a
disgusted exposure of so 'typically Lutheran' an immorality.
Since this procedure has been chosen even by outstanding
writers who are rightly regarded as authorities, it is only
natural that the falsity should have been repeated, probably
often in perfect innocence, by lesser writers.

Monogamy was the normal thing among Christians and
nobody in Henry VIII's time, with the exception of the Anabaptists of Münster (1534), denied its normality. Neither the
Pope nor Luther regarded bigamy as *desideratum*; but both
of them, and not they alone, regarded it as the lesser evil
compared with divorce.

Erasmus of Rotterdam gave, quite casually, the same
advice. He was drawn into Henry's affair in 1526 when
Catherine requested of him, through her chamberlain Lord
Mountjoy, that he should come to her aid by writing in her
favour. The result was the book *Matrimonii Christiani Insti-
tutio* in which the problems of divorce and impediments are
discussed at length; the book maintains that a marriage with
a deceased brother's wife does not, as such, present a cause
for nullification. During 1527 Erasmus was in correspondence
with Vives and the King's divorce affair was being discussed.
On September 2nd Erasmus wrote: 'Far be it from me to mix
in the affair of Jupiter and Juno, particularly as I know little
about it. But I should prefer that he should take two Junos
rather than put away one.'[89]

The mere fact that the Pope, Luther and Erasmus considered bigamy to be the obvious preferable solution indicates clearly that this idea, so alien and unacceptable to the
modern mind, was a perfectly reasonable reaction at the time.
Among those who had no scruples were also, for instance, the
French ambassador, the King of France (who in April 1532
said to Chapuys that the King should go ahead and marry the
lady of his choice as Louis XII had done in 1499; again in
January 1533 he advised Henry, through du Bellay, that he
should marry Anne without hesitation and afterwards defend
his cause) and Lord Wiltshire. The Pope, when discussing
the possibility of a marriage between Princess Mary and the
Duke of Norfolk's son, was aware of the fact that the Earl of
Surrey had a wife living; this, in the Pope's opinion, was not

too important as he had been forced into the marriage.[90] Erasmus is particularly well suited to show that the proposal of bigamy was not regarded as shocking; had he felt that he could be taken to task for proposing an immoral solution, he would never have given such an opinion in a letter written to England. Erasmus was not a courageous man. Indeed, after 1531, when he realized the course that events were taking, he no longer complied with the wishes of Queen Catherine, who again asked him for help at that time; he hedged and tiptoed precisely as he had done twelve years earlier when he was asked to state whether he was for or against Luther. Soon afterwards the necessity for caution had vanished, and then Erasmus dedicated some of his books to Lord Rochford—Anne Boleyn's father! No, Erasmus was hardly the kind of person to shock his correspondents. He always swam with the current. When advocating bigamy as a lesser evil than divorce, he simply expressed contemporary opinion.

Henry VIII and Philip of Hesse were by no means the only exalted persons who had given cause for such discussions and decisions. The Pope had permitted the King of Castile to have two wives.[91] Charles Brandon, Duke of Suffolk, Henry VIII's brother-in-law, committed bigamy twice, was three times divorced and finally married his daughter-in-law;[92] his case, one is happy to say, was not typical of the age, but it shows what was possible.

We have already mentioned that it was originally Henry VIII's opinion that a second marriage would be the solution of his problem and his first application to Clement VII requested papal permission for a second wife.[93] Soon afterwards he changed his mind and began to aim at a declaration of nullity, not—we repeat—because he judged bigamy to be immoral, but in consideration of the succession. Eventually, he hastily reverted to the original plan by marrying Anne Boleyn without being divorced from Catherine and, once again, it was consideration for the succession which prompted him, not that he regarded bigamy as the lesser evil.

The decision of Luther and his colleagues regarding Henry's matrimonial cause will be quoted later. Their memorandum will demonstrate, in the form of an extremely detailed investigation, by what reasoning bigamy was judged to

be incomparably less sinful than divorce, that bigamy was
considered at least possible whereas divorce was not; it is
therefore not necessary at this moment to discuss the theological argument. The point of the present paragraph is to indicate that no historian should feel compelled to improve on
reality by electing to treat the Pope's advice with discreet
silence—as if it had been immoral advice!—and by compen-
sating for this silence with rhetorical references to the scandal of Philip of Hesse. I have never been able to understand
how it is that so many historians outside the Roman obedience take a greater interest in damaging Luther's reputation
than in guarding their own.

Luther's attitude towards the problem of bigamy is made
clear in his reply to an inquiry; in 1526 he wrote to Joseph
Levin Metzsch: 'In answer to your question whether someone could marry more than one wife, this is my reply: un-
believers may do what they like, but Christian liberty must
be made to harmonize with charitable care for the welfare
of others wherever it can be done without harm to faith and
conscience. But nowadays everyone wants the sort of liberty
which pleases his own interest, without any care for the interest and improvement of the community. . . . Even if in the
olden days men had many wives, Christians should not
follow their example; they have no need to do so, it does not
improve them and there is no command to that effect in God's
word. Only scandal and disquiet would be the result. . . .'[94]

'Scandal and disquiet' were certainly not wanting when
Luther and Melanchthon granted, in December 1539, a
dispensation to Philip of Hesse to contract a second marriage.
Here, as in the matrimonial cause of Henry VIII, was a case
of a 'disturbed conscience'. The prince had led to excess the
kind of dissolute life which was practically the normal thing
among princes (Charles V by no means excepted), was badly
afflicted with syphilis and, somehow or other, full of certainty
that a second marriage would bring peace to his life; quite
possibly, he also hoped superstitiously for a miraculous cure
of the disease through a lawful union with a pure virgin.
Martin Bucer was sent to Wittenberg and Luther became
convinced that Philip's cause was a genuine conscientious
problem. The dispensation was granted. Long preambles
stated that monogamy was the normal divine institution; thus

it had been at the time of the creation and later became the laudable law in the Church despite the fact that in some eras concessions had become customary. This said, they proceeded to explain the possibility of an exception provided it was understood that there was a fundamental difference between the introduction of a new law or custom and the granting of a special dispensation. They implored the prince to keep the dispensation a close secret, for two reasons: firstly, it must not be presumed by anybody that a new custom had been sanctioned and, secondly, the opponents of the Lutherans should be prevented from hearing of it as they would, no doubt, broadcast the news that the Lutherans had become like the Anabaptists, or even like the Turks.

There follows a strong admonition that henceforth the prince must give up his adulteries, and a reminder (I Cor. vi, 9, 10) that according to St. Paul adulterers shall not enter into the Kingdom of Heaven. The letter further stresses that one of the chief duties of pastors is to guard the sanctity of matrimony and to keep a watch on all human institutions lest they become severed from their original and divinely ordained meaning. 'However, since your Grace finds it impossible to abstain from an unchaste life—you say that to do so is not possible to you—we should wish to see you in a better estate before God, enabling you to live henceforth with a quiet conscience for your Grace's own salvation and for the good of your land and people.'

Only a few months later the secret began, of course, to leak out. Luther at first thought it could be met by a denial, but this was no way out: the affair became common knowledge. Luther, not normally easily distressed about a wrong move if it was open to rectification, was full of regret and made no secret of this when writing to the quite despairing Melanchthon. 'The serpent and the serpent's brood of wisdom after the event will plague us more than all enemies and opponents have ever done.' He maintained that the devil's own wisdom had guided them when they granted the dispensation.

It was probably the scandal made of the case of Philip of Hesse which brought to an end the possibility of considering bigamy the lesser evil in comparison with the break-up of a matrimonial bond. Bigamy became as impossible as 'divorce' and the case of Philip, no doubt, strengthened the effect of Charles V's recent legislation against bigamy.

We have mentioned cases of dispensations for bigamy which caused no great scandal; they had been granted under the old religion. Here, however, was a case which called forth an ostentatious outcry against the rotten morals of the reformers. *Quod licet Jovi non licet bovi.* As a pastoral, individual dispensation, Luther's consent had been quite legitimate; diplomatically speaking—Luther had never pretended to be a diplomat, or to be guided by the morals of diplomats —the granting of the dispensation had been a gigantic blunder. The case of Philip of Hesse became—and has remained, when suitably told—the favourite subject for the portrayal of Luther the Knave.

Luther had no reason to regard the cases of Henry VIII and Philip of Hesse as in any way related. Philip's conscience was concerned with the conduct of his life; Henry VIII's conscience was troubled by the discovery that a marriage which had become burdensome had possibly never been a marriage. Philip wanted a second wife; Henry wanted a separation. Philip sent Bucer to Wittenberg with a pastoral question; Henry VIII sent delegations of experts on the Mosaic law. There is, altogether, little basis for comparison.

3

We return to the development of Henry's affairs. All references to the papal private advice that Henry should go ahead and marry Anne Boleyn as a second wife were invariably written in cipher in the dispatches of the ambassadors. The reason was not, as we have seen, that the suggestion, dubious no doubt, had the stigma of immorality but simply a precaution against the danger that Queen Catherine might hear of it and spoil the chance.

Henry VIII, as we have seen, was averse to taking the advice because only a declaration of nullity would serve to clarify the succession. The Pope was hesitant because he had to consider the imperial reaction should his personal advice to Henry become known to Charles V. The ambassadors re-

jected the Pope's advice, saying that they did not know
whether it would satisfy the King's conscience.[95] All this came
to an end in October 1530. The Pope then still cherished the
bigamy solution but now 'doubtfully; soon he retracted to
saying that he had been told by a great doctor he might [dis-
pense in that case], for the avoidance of greater scandal; but
he would advise further with his council'. And then, at long
last: 'Lately he has said plainly that he cannot do it.'[96]

Henry VIII was thus no nearer his aim to secure not papal
private advice but an official papal declaration—precisely the
thing he could not obtain from the Pope. It has been suggested that the Pope's hesitation to oblige Henry VIII was
due to his conscientious misgivings, not to his fear of Charles
V. 'The Holy See was never so corrupt as to pass untrue decisions for mere political reasons.'[97] It is a question whether
the case of Henry VIII is a particularly suitable example to
bear out this statement.

In December 1530 the Pope reverted to strong interference.
A consistorial decree issued at Rome requested that the Archbishop of Canterbury should be prohibited from taking the
cognizance of the cause and also barred Henry from co-
habiting with any other woman except Catherine and forbidding all women to contract marriage with the King of
England.[98] This was followed, on January 5th, 1531, by a new
papal decree forbidding the laity as well as the clergy, universities, parliaments and courts of law from dealing with the
case.[99] All this constituted conflict with English sovereignty,
although the King's request for a dispensation from the ruling
of a papal dispensation (that of 1503) was, naturally, a papal
prerogative. However, such strong papal 'interference' made
it possible to rouse English national self-respect to utter
protests. Although these were duly announced, Henry still
entertained hopes that the Pope might yet yield to his demand. In the meantime, he tried again to obtain Catherine's
consent to have the cause tried in England. On March 31st,
1531, a deputation of lords and bishops descended upon her,
taking her by surprise at a late hour when she was bound to
be without advisers. The deputation suggested to her that it
was entirely her responsibility that Henry had been cited to
Rome, that she must see the indignity of it and give consent
that a mutually chosen group of judges, who were beyond

suspicion of partiality, should try the case in England. However, the Queen refused to be outwitted; since her case was
infinitely stronger than that of the King, she managed quite
easily to hold her ground against the formidable assembly
and the deputation had to withdraw without having achieved
anything.[100]

It is impossible to say how long Henry might have continued his persistent attempts to persuade the Pope to decide
in his favour. It might well have gone on for many more years
but for the emergence of an entirely new situation which
prompted Henry to substitute speed and action for a continuation of the time-consuming negotiations: by the end of
January 1533 Henry knew that Anne Boleyn was pregnant,
and towards the end of the month he married her secretly.
The child's legitimacy was at stake and no quick decision
from Rome could be hoped for. Therefore the Archbishop of
Canterbury had to be given authority to pronounce a decision, his court had to be recognized quickly as the supreme
tribunal for English ecclesiastical cases. Special circumstances
made it easy just then to convert the plan into reality because
Archbishop Warham had died in August 1532 and the See
of Canterbury was still vacant. The only problem was speed
and secrecy and to find the right man for the job. Henry had
a swift idea of his immediate programme. Cranmer was notified of his election as Archbishop while he was abroad as
the King's ambassador to Charles V. He was urged to return
immediately and he arrived in England in January. On March
30th he was consecrated, and on April 11th he asked the King
for gracious permission to determine the cause of the divorce,
'because much bruit exists among the comon people on
the subject'.[101] This petition had been carefully edited and
amended by the King who then haughtily indicated his gracious consent, although he could not recognize any superior
on earth. Two days earlier, on April 9th, Catherine was told
that the marriage had taken place. The news was revealed to
her after an argument with the Duke of Norfolk who had
been sent to her to make her relinquish her title. It was Lord
Mountjoy who told her afterwards that, indeed, she was to
be known henceforth as the Princess of Wales. On April 12th
Anne appeared for the first time openly as queen.

On May 10th Cranmer opened his court at Dunstable.

be marueyled at / if any pzince oz kyng
fauour ŷ gospell / and I desyze with
all my hert inwardly / that I may o=
nes haue cause to reioyce ⁊ make con
gratulatyon of this myzacle in your
highnesse / and I pray god / by whose
fauour and assistēce I wzite this let=
ter / that he so wozke with my wozdſ /
that the kynge of Englande may be
made shoztly / the perfyte discyple of
Chzist and pzofessour of the gospell /
and finally / most benigne lozde vnto
Luther. Amen. Some ansf were / if
it may lyke your highnesse I loke af
ter / mylde and benigne: At Wyttem=
burch / the fyzste day of Septembze /
the yere of our lozde / a . M̃. D. xxb.

Most humble subiecte vnto
your regall maiesty / Mar=
tyn Luther / his owne hāde.

The an=

V and VI. The King's reply to Luther's offer of an apology of 1525
(1526). The end of Luther's letter and (overleaf) the opening of
Henry VIII's answer.

¶ The answere of the most mighty ⁊ noble prince kyng Hēry the. viii. kyng of Englāde ⁊ of Fraūce/ defēsor of the fayth and lorde of Irelāde/ vnto the letters of Martyn Luther.

Our letters wrytten the fyrst day of Septembre/ we haue receyued the. xx. day of Marche: In whiche ye write your selfe/to be sorie and ashamed/ that ye folyly ⁊ hastely/ nat of your owne mynde : but by the instygation of other/ suche as lytell fauoured me/dyd put out your boke agaist me/with whiche ye knowe your selfe that ye haue sore offended me/ And therfore haue cause to be i drede and

B   shame

Catherine was called upon to give evidence but she refused to obey the summons as, naturally, she did not recognize the jurisdiction of Cranmer's court. Sentence was pronounced on May 23rd. The Pope, it was decided, had no power to grant such dispensations as the one given to Henry VII in 1503 for his son, and in consequence Henry VIII and Catherine of Aragon had never been married. Five days afterwards a declaration followed from Lambeth announcing that Henry VIII and Anne Boleyn were legally married. On June 1st Anne Boleyn's coronation took place in Westminster Abbey. The child was born on September 7th. It was a girl—the future Queen Elizabeth.

It had all been pointless so far: Henry VIII was still without a male heir. It is easy to imagine the dreadful disappointment, and it may well be that the King's bitter resentment played an important part in his future attitudes. For the time being he was forced to continue in his indomitable hope for male issue. Meanwhile, no doubt in anticipation of the fulfilment of this hope, the birth of the daughter enabled him to deprive Mary of the title 'Princess' and to transfer it to Elizabeth. As far as this went, the King gained at least the satisfaction of demonstrating the marvellous legality of the achievement. Of course, not everybody shared this conviction. Queen Catherine was not impressed by the disreputable apparatus which had added the lustre of legal correctness to Henry's clever manœuvre. Quite apart from the transparent falsehood of the whole proceedings, Cranmer's court had based its decision on an argument with which she could on no count agree. In March 1533 Convocation had decided—against Catherine's repeated solemn word—that her first marriage had been consummated.

The Pope reacted in July 1533—a little late, surely—by reaffirming the validity of Henry's marriage with Catherine. He may have had certain premonitions when he had been asked to confirm the choice of Cranmer as Archbishop; very reluctantly he granted his consent, in due consideration of Henry's threat to withhold the offerings of first-fruits from the English benefices. The one thing which the Pope had certainly not foreseen was Henry's most clever stroke: the *Statute in Restraint of Appeals* of March 1533, although even this was not altogether a surprise; in May 1532 Henry VIII

G

had delivered an address to the Speaker and twelve members of the Commons, in which he said that he considered the clergy to be only half his subjects because of their oath to the Pope.[102]

It was too late now for the Pope to intervene effectively. From 1534 Henry VIII extended to other fields his successful experiment with ecclesiastical independence of Rome. The decision of Cranmer's court had relieved him of his troubled conscience in the matter of his cohabitation with Catherine of Aragon. As far as he was concerned, the matrimonial cause was over, although he still needed the approval of important outsiders that he had done the right thing. Meanwhile what had hitherto served exclusively the quick progress of the divorce, was now used to inaugurate a Church reformation. In 1534 Convocation decided that the Pope had no jurisdiction (within the realm of England) conferred upon him by God in the Holy Scriptures (at that time an argument with Lutheran associations). This was declared on March 31st. Three days afterwards, the submission of the clergy was confirmed by a parliamentary Act. There followed further Acts abolishing annates and the Peter's pence; Campeggio and Ghinucci were deprived of their English bishoprics; the Archbishop of Canterbury was invested with the power to grant licences and dispensations which had hitherto been papal prerogatives.

An Act of Parliament was published which settled the succession on Anne Boleyn's children. Henry VIII had the impudence to ask even Catherine, together with her retinue, to take the oath that she would respect this Act; he probably did not really expect her to comply, but his object was to deprive her of all servants unwilling to take the oath. He answered Catherine's refusal by threatening her with execution and by placing her under house arrest, but under pressure from Chapuys he had to give way on this point.

4

The sketch given of Henry's negotiations with Rome in the divorce affair and of his eventual solution of the problem may suffice, despite all the obvious shortcomings of so brief a summary, to show that the significance of Henry's attempts to obtain a favourable verdict from Luther should not be overestimated. It was only one of very many schemes. Throughout his dealings with those whom he invited to give an opinion on the cause, he maintained that his fundamental motive was a troubled conscience; a message from Henry VIII to Charles V in 1529 said, 'he could not quiet his conscience remaining longer with the queen, whom for her nobleness of blood and other virtues, he had loved entirely as his wife until he saw that their union was forbidden in Scripture. Unless, therefore, he would willingly destroy his soul, there are so many reasons to persuade the dissolution of the marriage, that he cannot abide it.'[103]

We have seen that it was not quite as simple as that. The contemporary world, and most certainly the directly interested persons, knew very well that the troubled conscience may have been a contributory, perhaps even a prominent, motive, but a motive among others. The Pope was certainly primarily concerned with the political implications. But the whole proceedings had little of the atmosphere one would expect in an affair in which a penitent seeks to restore his peace of mind. Nobody, apart from Henry and his adherents, seems to have worried much about the state of the King's conscience. The universities treated the subject as a thesis well suited for scholastic hairsplitting, employing a time-honoured method by which, with some ingenuity, any desirable result could be achieved. The Lutherans treated the inquiry simply as a pastoral case and failed entirely to exploit it as a strong gesture against the Emperor, as Henry had probably hoped they would.

The significance of Henry's approach to Wittenberg has two aspects: Luther's very carefully considered answer is totally disinterested; and, secondly, the mere fact that Henry asked Luther for help, after all that had happened in 1521 and 1525, seems to indicate that the divorce was more important to him than what is generally presumed to be his unshakeable conviction that Luther was a heretic.

In 1526, answering Luther's offer of an apology, the King had written sarcastically that 'one or two freres apostates ron out of our Realme, raignying in riote and unthufty lyberte with

you of whome we reken our Realme so well rydd that if there
were any mo suche here (as we truste there may be nat many)
we wolde ye had them to'. In 1531, the idea occurred to
Henry that one could possibly use the good offices of these
English refugees, driven out of England by himself, to influence Luther. The choice fell on Robert Barnes who was
invited to return to England.

Barnes was born in 1495. He studied at Louvain, became
doctor of theology in 1523 and was thereafter the prior of the
Augustinians at Cambridge. He had early been attracted by
Luther's writings and his troubles began in 1525 after he had
preached a sermon on December 24th at St. Edmund's, Cambridge, which was blatantly Lutheran and quickly recognized
as heretical. He was charged, first before the Vice-Chancellor
and afterwards before Wolsey, on twenty-five points of
heresy. He insisted on defending himself; however, in the
course of the trial which lasted three days he recanted. It
appears that his Lutheran sympathies were quite deep-
rooted, as soon after his recantation he reverted to them. All
the same, he recanted again in 1539, that is whenever he was
confronted with direct accusation. The recantation of 1526
saved him from the stake, but he was not permitted to return
to Cambridge; he lived for a while in London, then at North-
ampton, but in 1528 he thought it advisable to leave England
for Antwerp. Soon he moved on to Wittenberg where he lived
in Bugenhagen's house.

While Barnes lived in exile, the Henrican reformation
began, as we have seen, in closest association with the development of the divorce proceedings. In the foregoing pages
we were exclusively concerned with the matrimonial cause.
We have seen that in 1531 the separation from the papacy was
put into effect in the greatest haste owing to Anne Boleyn's
pregnancy. In July of that year Henry said to Chapuys, when
refusing him permission to make a visitation of the Cistercian
monasteries, that he alone was King, Emperor and Pope as
far as English affairs were concerned.[104] The transition had
taken place with an astonishing smoothness and Henry had
found out, possibly to his own surprise, what could be
achieved in this respect. Not only had he succeeded in marrying Anne Boleyn and consolidating his power at home, 'the
recognition of the king in 1531 as supreme head on earth of

the Church of England was closely connected with the appropriation of £118,840 by the supreme head'. But the facility with which the Church parted with its money opened the supreme eyes a little wider. 'If they will pay, they will surrender power.'[105]

At the time when Barnes was invited to return to England, things were still in a state of flux. Characteristically, the invitation did not come from Henry himself but from Cromwell; it was conveyed to Barnes with conspiratorial secrecy. Not even Sir Thomas More knew of it; consequently, it so happened that upon hearing of Barnes's arrival, More—who was just at this time particularly active in prosecuting Lutheran heresy—attempted to imprison him, being in ignorance of the latest royal scheme.

Soon after his arrival in England, Barnes returned to Wittenberg. Through an agent whose identity is unknown, Henry VIII forwarded the verdicts of the universities to Barnes and the agent requested that Luther's opinion on these verdicts should be solicited. During the same year, Simon Grynaeus, a German humanist of international reputation, was asked to approach his friend Oecolompadius, also Zwingli, Bucer and others; Cranmer consulted Osiander (his uncle by marriage) who judged that the papal dispensation of 1503 was given unlawfully; he summarized his opinions in a thesis *De matrimonio incesto* which, however, was suppressed to prevent giving offence to Charles V.[106]

Robert Barnes knew Luther well and it is likely that he was more or less certain that Luther would take an unfavourable view of Henry's separation from Catherine. He paid a special visit to Philip of Hesse and asked him to influence Luther; the Duke complied and wrote to Luther accordingly, pointing out to him the possible political advantages of a favourable verdict. He wrote shortly before September 22nd and his letter arrived too late; by the time Luther received it, a negative reply had already been handed to Barnes. It is inconceivable that Philip's letter should have made the slightest difference.

Luther's decision is dated September 5th, 1531. It is so long and painstaking that in the following quotation some passages are given in summary. Square brackets indicate a condensed argument of omitted paragraphs. The letter is

addressed to Dr. Barnes who, while living in Germany, had
adopted the name Antonius Anglus.

Luther wrote:

'We have already had private conversations and friendly
discussions concerning the cause of the king of England, my
Anthony, and as you know, this is my opinion: I like best the
decision given by the university of Louvain and consider it
preferable to all those others which are contrary to it. The
king could follow its advice with a clear conscience and
indeed must do so before God. That is to say, on no account
can he separate himself from the queen (his brother's wife)
whom he has truly married; he may not, by means of such a
divorce, taint the name of both the daughter and the mother
with the shame of incest. I am not writing of the dispensation
of the Roman pope which permitted the marriage with the
wife of his deceased brother. But this I will say: if we consider
that the king may have sinned through his marriage with the
wife of his late brother, then it would be a far greater and
heavier sin to throw her off now that he has really taken her,
and to rend the bond of marriage in so cruel a manner; to do
so would be to cover himself, and also the queen and the
princess, with the everlasting shame of impurity and incest.
In point of fact, there is no reason why they should be slan-
dered with so extraordinary an accusation, nor why they
should, in addition, suspend the marriage; which two sins
are certainly so dreadful that the former, lesser sin which,
furthermore, is already absolved, and therefore no longer sin,
cannot be compared with them. For, the matrimonial union
of husband and wife is safeguarded by divine and by human
law. But, the prohibition against marrying the wife of a
deceased brother only belongs to the human law, not to the
divine, unless one maintains the notion that all laws are
divine, all of them being good before God.

'Those who advise the king in favour of divorce bring great
trouble to his conscience. Nay, they sin against the divine
law. If they quote from Lev. xviii that it is against God's
will to marry a deceased brother's wife, *Thou shalt not un-
cover the nakedness of thy brother's wife; it is thy brother's
nakedness*, then this is my answer. If they wish to enforce the
Mosaic law and submit us to this legislator, then they will

only achieve this conclusion: not only would the king be obliged to retain the queen, having married her, he would have been obliged to marry her, had he not already done so, in order *to raise seed unto his brother* because his deceased brother had no children from his wife; this we find distinctly said in Deut. xxv and the Sadducees repeated it before Christ, Matt. xxii.

'Now, here they say that the law in Deut. xxv was merely an ecclesiastical law which must give way to the moral law in Lev. xviii, because the ceremonial law has been dissolved whereas the moral laws have remained, and so on. Surely all must see that such glossators are either partial, or else talk thoughtlessly and untruthfully. But if they really found such a gloss, could one not find yet another one which would contradict the law of Lev. xviii? The fact is, in the first case they wanted a gloss and here they did not want one. It is therefore clear that they did not approach with an unbiased judgment a law which was disagreeable to them, but were satisfied with law making glosses which harmonized with their wishes.

'Next, how could they prove that the law in Deut. xxv is, and always was, only a ceremonial law, particularly if it is their intentions to quiet the king's conscience? This is how we like it and therefore we maintain that it is an ecclesiastical law. On the contrary, we say that the law in Deuteronomy was truly a moral law, because it does indeed belong to the laws of society; it was introduced to protect the family, to safeguard inheritance, in a word: for the protection and welfare of the community. Just as one must cultivate the fields in this or that season, by a variety of means, in order to increase the growth of fruit, so this is truly a law of society and morals promoting the well-being of individual houses as well as the whole country. Therefore the Jews had to obey this law no less than all other peoples. And the text shows clearly that it deals with the preservation of families and heirs; it is therefore not a ceremonial, but a necessary and social law.

'Even if we regarded the law of Deuteronomy as a moral law, what has it to do with the problem under discussion? Under Moses, the Jews had to obey this law, just as they had to be circumcized and obey other customs. Now, let them explain to us how it is that the Jews can marry their deceased

brothers' wives if it was forbidden by divine law in Lev.
xviii. After all, these two laws stand in clear conflict with
each other, if they are understood as relating to the deceased
brother. It is therefore obvious that they neither understand
the words nor the persons of which the law speaks.

'If they maintain that the ceremonial law has been abrogated and that the moral law has remained and that, therefore, the law of Deuteronomy is not to be observed, but that of
Leviticus remains intact, then, firstly, it is obvious that the Jews
have observed both laws, as I have said before. Therefore
they must needs agree that the Jews did not offend against
Leviticus by observing the law of Deuteronomy. Next, there is
their argument that the ceremonial law had been abrogated
because it is bad and forbidden for us. I will answer: it is not
sufficient to quote a conflicting law from Leviticus, they must
demonstrate that the quoted law is no longer in force. But
now, they build up their argument with other laws at the
same time as they maintain the abrogation of certain laws;
but they go to great trouble to cite certain laws and maintain
the significance of Moses in order to persuade others that
they are right. Their method shows that they choose such
round-about ways not from the love of truth but from the
desire to overcome difficulties. They argue with subterfuges
which Aristotle calls a *non causa ad causam*.

'Inasmuch as in the time of Moses the law of Deuteronomy
was still in force, it is not possible to make use either of the
abrogation of laws nor of conflicting laws in order to decide
a cause; both were still in force. The proof deduced from the
conflict between the laws is therefore quite invalid. If there
is anything left to examine, then it is the abrogation; however, in that case they can on no account enforce the opposing
law in Leviticus.

'Now those who think that the ceremonial law is forbidden
do not seem to us to understand at all what is implied by
abrogation, or the term "ceremonial".... [Here Luther illus-
trates the meaning by discoursing about the circumcision.]

'Now, the true interpretation is, that the levitical law deals
with the wife of a brother still alive and the law in Deuteronomy with the wife of a deceased brother ... Thus also John
the Baptist punished Herod because he had taken the wife
of a brother who was still alive....

'Can one not conclude from Deuteronomy that it would be possible for someone to marry his own daughter? That after Othniel's death, his wife having left Achse the daughter of Caleb, Caleb—being Othniel's brother—would have been forced to marry his own daughter? This shows how easy it is through such elaborations to argue in favour of an evil cause. It is just as if they did not know that a higher law dissolves a lesser law . . . [Luther demonstrates this by the example of the Jewish problem of whether circumcision could be done on a Sabbath day and adds that in common practice royal laws stand above local laws and rules laid down by the master of the house.]

'But what is the use, my Anthony, of so long a treatise, if in the future you have to deal with people who cannot understand the laws? Let us come nearer to the case actually under discussion and say that Moses is dead for us, but that he lived for the Jews, and his laws are not obligatory for us. That is why we do not accept anything from Moses in his capacity as a legislator, unless it can be shown to be in agreement with our moral and political laws; we do not wish to see all the nations of the world in confusion; we desire to avoid like poison any disregard for, and corruption of, laws. Those laws may have applied to their nation, but we have our own legislators for such cases. Therefore it must be understood that if the marriage between a man and his deceased brother's wife is forbidden according to the laws of the pope or of the emperor, then the following questions are raised: is the king obliged to abstain from marrying the queen forbidden to him? Or, if they are already married, must he divorce her? And here the answer must be: "No". On the contrary, on pain of eternal condemnation he must keep her. . . . [Here, Luther once again expounds the laws of the Old Testament.]

'The King of England has sinned by taking the wife of his deceased brother, but it was only a sin under human and social law deriving from the pope and the emperor. If then the pope and the emperor granted a dispensation from their own law, then he has not sinned. For, if God approves of the emperor's social laws, He also approves of an imperial law granted by the emperor. . . . And as for the capacity of the pope as a secular ruler, since he does not legislate by right, his dispensation is even more binding than his legislation. If the king throws off the queen, he would commit a very grave sin against the law of God which says: *what God has joined together, no man shall put asunder* . . . [Luther argues that the King is not permitted to set man-made laws above the law of God.]

'Now, Anthony, you have my opinion. I cannot tell whether it is advisable to publish it now. It may well be possible that my name would do harm to the cause; you well know how hated and abominated it is. Thus, it may well be possible that hatred of my name might lead to a rejection of my verdict, even if the judgment I have given is sound. I will leave it to you to take council with good friends about my verdict and then to decide whether you should suppress it or make it known. I earnestly wish, were it not for the hatred of my name, that my opinion would be of use to the king and to the queen, in order to prevent their being led astray into that godless and illegal divorce which will only serve to give them a guilty conscience for ever.

'Eventually it may well happen that the king, either by himself or in accordance with the advice of other doctors, will carry out the divorce; should that happen, you should still endeavour to persuade your friends that they should express their disapproval of the divorce. Even if the king is wholly misled by adversaries, still we should at least do all that is possible to protect the queen, so that she may under no circumstances consent to the divorce, being willing to die rather than to burden her conscience with so great an evil before God. She should believe implicitly that she is the true and legitimate queen of England, ordained and confirmed before God. For, she must never be allowed to burden herself with an invented evil or consider a great sin what is in fact no sin at all. To do so would be to worship with awe the fancies of a wandering conscience in the place of God. If, God forbid, the king cannot be preserved from this evil, the queen's soul must still be saved so that she may bear as her cross the misfortune imposed on her with such gross injustice, even if the divorce cannot be prevented. Only, she must never give her consent to it.

'I, who can do nothing else, call upon God in my prayer that Christ may prevent this divorce and that he may put to naught the temptations of Ahitophel who defends the divorce. Or, if it is not His will to prevent it, then may He grant to the queen strong faith, constancy and a sure conscience so that she may be and for ever remain the legal and true queen of England despite all that may happen and in the face of all the powers of hell and of the world, Amen.

'As to yourself, farewell in Christ.

Wittenberg, 1531 on the 5th of September.

D. Martin Luther'[107]

5

Dr. Barnes returned to England immediately with this answer which was, obviously, far from pleasing to Henry VIII. Since Luther's reply could only be understood as showing a definite, considered opinion and since, in addition, the relationship between the King and Luther had not been cordial in the past, one would have expected Henry to give up any further hopes of winning a Lutheran approval of the divorce. Nevertheless, having worried the Pope for many years in this affair with ever-renewed attempts, the King was not ready to relinquish his demands on the Wittenbergers so quickly. The very day after Barnes's arrival in England, Paget was dispatched to open new negotiations with the Protestant princes and there followed further attempts in 1532, 1534 and 1535–1536.

In one respect, the mission of Robert Barnes to Luther in 1531 is quite different from the later negotiations. It was similar to all the other steps which Henry had taken in order to solicit favourable verdicts from universities, canonists, Jews and reformers, since he was exclusively concerned with the matrimonial cause. But from 1532 onwards the divorce was no longer the sole object, at times not even the most important point, of Henry's negotiations with the Lutherans.

Here it remains to point out that Luther did, in principle, object strongly to a marriage of the kind which Henry VIII had contracted, by papal dispensation, with Catherine of Aragon. In 1535 his advice was sought in the following case: someone had had intercourse with his deceased wife's sister

and wished to marry her. Luther, Justus Jonas and Melanchthon replied together in a memorandum which entirely opposed the projected marriage which they considered forbidden both by God's law (Lev. xviii) and by imperial law
(*Codex de incestuosis et inutilibus nuptiis*). 'We are of the
opinion that these persons would never have a quiet conscience if they were married; beyond any doubt, they would
attain to a much greater peace of mind if they parted from
each other. . . . Since these people will be in great trouble
because of the sin and the shame, and also on account of their
friendship towards each other, you must comfort them with
the Gospel and make it clear to them that they would always
suffer from a troubled conscience if they were married, for
the reasons stated above. It would be easier to comfort them
if they parted company immediately. . . .'[108]

To conclude this subject, a further quotation from Luther
might indicate in a general way his awareness of the great
difficulties involved in the settlement of matrimonial causes.
This derives from a memorandum written by the same three
Wittenberg theologians, Luther, Jonas and Melanchthon,
relating to the negotiations in 1531 between the Protestant
princes and the Electors of Mainz and the Palatinate:

'If the bishops will continue to assume jurisdiction in
matrimonial causes, not only will we not complain, but we
will consider it gladly and willingly; since it is distressing
and dangerous work and it might well happen in the future
that we would make decisions as wrong as theirs. Since our
age is so full of sectarian spirits, and of many other difficult
problems, which may be on the increase still, we shall be
glad to free ourselves as far as possible, as we have anyway
enough work on our hands.

'What we have taught and said about the *gradibus* was not
done because we desired to introduce new laws and rules;
we only wished to give comfort and assurance to the conscience of persons who cannot attain such certainty through
papal dispensations, or who are otherwise burdened by such
laws. They must not think that there could ever be a case
when a marriage ought to be dissolved for God's sake, or that
they could leave each other because of man-made laws. The
purpose of our whole teaching is always to give guidance to
troubled, imprisoned and disturbed consciences that they

may share in Christian truth and liberty. This is by no means a concession to the rough populace; on the contrary, we put them under strictest laws and there they will remain; we do not invite them to use as easy rights such comfort and liberty, *ne libertas detur in offendiculum eorum.*'[108]

Part IV

NEW APPROACHES TO WITTENBERG AND
FINAL ALIENATION

1

THE previous Part of this book opened with a summary sketch of the matrimonial conflict in order to provide a general background of the subsequent negotiations with Luther and his circle concerning the divorce. This chapter, too, will have to contain brief surveys. The vast bulk of the negotiations between Henry VIII and the German Protestant princes in the period between 1535 and 1540 do not belong to our subject proper, which is restricted to the personal relations between Henry and Luther. While the King was, of course, very actively taking part in these enterprises, Luther had little to do with them. His pronounced scepticism regarding Henry VIII developed into frank contempt after a brief moment of optimism.

Henry VIII's dealings with the League of Schmalkald have been examined minutely by the German historian S. Prüser whose important book on the subject has unaccountably remained untranslated.[109] The theological implications of these approaches have received some attention, by no means exhaustive, from G. E. Rupp, the foremost English Lutheran scholar of our time,[110] and, from the Catholic point of view, from Philip Hughes.[111]

As we have pointed out, Henry VIII's attempts to obtain from Luther a favourable verdict in the matrimonial cause did not by any means imply an approach to Lutheranism, even though it was made at the time of the beginning of Henry's reformation. In point of fact, the year 1531 was particularly difficult for Lutheran sympathizers in England. Christopher van Endhoven, a printer from Antwerp, died in Westminster prison where he had been sent for selling copies of Tyndale's New Testament. Bayfield, who had consistently imported Lutheran books, was burned at Smithfield. In the

H

same year Bilney and John Tewkesbury went to the stake.
G. Constantine was released because he disclosed to Sir
Thomas More the names of his companions, particularly those
of his shipping contacts; after his release he became registrar
to the Bishop of St. David's, one of More's accusers. During
the following two years there were further burnings of heretics. While Henry VIII's ambassadors visited the Lutherans
on the King's behalf, Sir Thomas More, undoubtedly with the
King's approval, sustained a more determined effort than
ever to root out Lutheran influence in England. Inconsistency
of this kind accompanied Henry's ecclesiastical policy at
almost all its stages and one must not let one's own partiality
influence one's judgment as to which of the contradictory
policies represented Henry's true concern. Here, as elsewhere, it seems that the course of events was settled simply
by the opportunity and expediency of the moment. Many
a scheme in Henry's career was conceived when the time was
propitious and put into practice only when changes in the
situation had made it undesirable; very frequently the lapse
of a few weeks sufficed to introduce such changes of direction
and, in their train, new instances of duplicity.

The next series of negotiations began on the very day when
Barnes returned to England with Luther's negative verdict
on the King's divorce. It was marked first by Henry's resolute
intention yet to secure the Lutherans' approval of the divorce,
secondly by his desire to join the Schmalkald League of Protestant princes, and lastly by the necessity, arising from the
development of the Henrican reformation, of examining the
Lutheran theology from a new point of view. In the matter
of the divorce, the King's mind was as undivided as ever;
twelve years had passed since he had first begun to convince
himself and the world that it was his religious and moral
duty to separate himself from Catherine, and one can presume that at least he himself had no longer any doubts about
his fine rectitude in the dubious affair. Regarding the Schmalkald League, Henry's attitude varied between keen enthu-
siasm when threatened with isolation, and detached indifference when other affiliations seemed open to him. From
Lutheran teachings he hoped to be able to pick and choose,
to accept whatever suited his aims to refute the Pope's authority in England and to reject whatever appeared to him an

unnecessary and uncongenial doctrinal change. It is interesting to compare the exploitation of Lutheran teaching for the
dissolution of the monasteries (which was advantageous to
the King) with the arguments put forward in favour of the
celibacy of priests (which had no political or financial implication).

2

The League of Schmalkald came into being in the course of
defensive discussions among the German Protestant princes
relating to the jurisdiction of the imperial courts which constantly harassed them. This led to a renewed examination of
the problem of whether or not resistance to the Emperor
was permissible. In addition, there was the important issue
of Archduke Ferdinand's election as King of Rome; not only
the Protestants objected, but also the Catholic Bavarian
princes who wanted that crown for one of their own group.
This caused the Bavarians to approach the leaders of the
Protestant League, particularly Philip of Hesse, and the outcome was, in October 1531, a treaty which greatly strengthened the League. Gradually it became a formidable political
power. In May 1532 a treaty was made with France, and,
strangely enough, the League became of interest to none other
than the Pope himself whose 'indissoluble friendship and
treaty' with Charles V had just come to an end. The Emperor
unceasingly urged the Pope to call a general council, and
committed an infringement of papal territorial rights by con-
ceding to the Duke of Ferrara the possession of Modena
and Reggio. Such developments, together with the constant
Turkish threat, led to consultations in Rome early in 1531,
and again in April 1532, as to whether it would not be advisable to make a few concessions to the Lutherans such as the
permission for priests to marry, or the administration of the
chalice to the laity and so forth. This led eventually to very
serious negotiations, strongly supported by Francis I, between Cardinal du Bellay and the Lutherans. At the request
of the Bishop of Paris, Melanchthon drew up articles for discussion; these contained formidable concessions on the part of
the Lutherans. After the death of Clement, Paul III showed

himself no less interested. These negotiations led to an invitation to Melanchthon, by Francis I, to visit France and this, as we shall see, stirred Henry VIII into action.

We can here only indicate the endless entanglements in the diplomatic history of the period. They include, for instance, the treaties made between Charles V and the Protestants in 1532 at Ratisbon and Nuremberg; the marriage of Clement VII's niece with the second son of Francis; the agreement made between the Pope and Francis at Marseilles in 1533.

Another circle of intricate diplomatic policy had its centre at Lübeck where the burgomaster Jürgen Wullenwever had established a powerful democratic regime with the aim of renewing Lübeck's strong commercial position in the north. This led to the decline of the Hanse. Here, Henry VIII was deeply involved through his assistance to Wullenwever, particularly in the matter of new troubles caused in Denmark by encouragements from Lübeck; he was actually at one point offered the Danish crown.

Henry VIII watched the unsettled scene of the diplomatic world, so fraught with possibilities, in the hope of finding some opportunity of consolidating his own position which did not seem to benefit from any of the current developments. On the contrary; if a conciliation between Rome and the Lutherans were to succeed, he alone would remain in schism. Threatened with isolation, it became extremely important to him to prevent such a reconciliation and, simultaneously, to make some new and strong moves to gain an alliance with someone—if not with Francis I then perhaps with the Lutherans.

The relationship with Francis I had practically come to an end, but here Henry was able to continue for quite a time his favourite game of noncommittal approaches, characterized by mighty verbosity. There were days when the trick still worked, and other days when it did not. Generally speaking, Henry was no longer in alliance with anyone, a situation which inevitably resulted in the deterioration of trade and the withdrawal of investment by foreigners, and consequently in considerable unrest among the people.

3

In July 1533, when relations with Francis had reached a very
critical state, Stephen Vaughan, a friend of Cromwell's, was
sent to Germany to make alliances with various Lutheran
princes, but he soon found himself without definite instructions from home and without real knowledge of the King's
wishes; this uncertainty caused him many an unhappy day.
On September 25th he wrote to Cromwell pleading for instructions, since in this uncertainty 'I dare not do thone ne
other'. A whole month later he was still in the dark and
'excidyngly thyrst to know how the kynges Hieghnes takethe
my labours' (October 21st). In this letter he also told Cromwell how he conducted the King's overtures: 'I made light
therof, as thoughe the kyng sought theyr amities, not for his
necessitie, but muche more to do them good and pleasure. . . .
I purposed in no wyse to have my Prynces honour towched,
ne to shew that for any nede the kynges Hieghnes sought
them but rather so to compasse my matter, as thoughe it
shulde be apparaunt unto them that the kynges Hieghnes
onely sent me unto them to do them good.' Vaughan's task
was not an enviable one and it is understandable that he
should have ended his letter: 'If I have not shortly your
answere, yow kyll me.'[112] Soon afterwards he returned without any results whatsoever.

The negotiations with the Schmalkald League only reached
their climax in November 1535 when Barnes, Fox and Heath
were sent to Germany. There were careful preludes which
created the impression that Henry would consider acting as
the 'Defender of the League' if he were formally petitioned
to do so. At the same time, confusing news reached the German Lutherans about the King's reformation of the Church,
news which led them to believe that Henry had indeed made
approaches towards Protestantism in his realm. This news
was bound to be somewhat puzzling. During the year 1532,
persecution of heretics with Lutheran tendencies had continued in England. On the other hand, in the same year
Henry had caused the re-publication of Luther's apologetic
letter of 1525, together with his own declaration that the

late Cardinal Wolsey had caused all the strife between himself and Luther by persuading him to write against the *Babylonian Captivity of the Church* in 1521—precisely the theory which Henry had so heatedly rejected in his reply to Luther in 1527. This episode may have been a device to soften Luther in the matter of the matrimonial cause, but it failed to impress him and he simply declared to his English visitors over and over again that he had nothing further to say in the matter. However, the total impression made by Henry's persistent approaches to the Protestant princes and to the Wittenberg theologians actually led the Lutheran princes to write a 'petition' to Henry VIII to join their ranks. The King was as keen as ever to give the impression that his alliances were entirely due to magnanimous consideration of the humble approaches on the part of others.

Between 1531 and 1535 Luther was but little concerned with the affairs of Henry VIII. The earlier negotiations with the Schmalkald League were predominantly political and Luther was totally uninterested in politics. He did not become involved again until the summer of 1535. Barnes had just returned to England after one of his visits to Wittenberg when Henry learned that King Francis had furthered the negotiations between Rome and Wittenberg, and that he had issued the invitation to Philip Melanchthon to come to Paris. Promptly Barnes was dispatched back to Wittenberg to invite Melanchthon to come to England, instead of going to France. Barnes also conveyed 500 florins for Melanchthon and 50 florins for Luther as presents from the King. It is interesting to note that Henry was realistic enough not to waste much money on Luther.

Melanchthon's conciliatory nature, which caused two kings to seek his presence as a possible bridge to Luther, was sufficiently well known to the Elector John Frederick of Saxony for him to be apprehensive about the possible dangers. On August 19th, 1535, he wrote to his chancellor: 'We are truly concerned that . . . Philip might make many concessions if he went to France, which would not afterwards find the approval of Dr. Martinus and of the other theologians. . . . Apart from all this, there is actually no reason to believe that the French have a sincere concern for the Gospel; they presume that Philip will yield to pressure, that they could get hold of

him and make use of him.... In the end they will even pro-
claim that Philip approves of the false English marriage....'[113]

With the news that the French were inviting Melanchthon
to Paris, Henry VIII accelerated his efforts to impress the
Lutherans. So keen were his protestations that now even
Luther began to consider the possibility that the King's intentions might be sincere. Robert Barnes was on his way to
Saxony and on September 12th Luther wrote to Chancellor
Brück: '... the present overtures of the King to accept the
Gospel and to join the league of our princes and also to establish the Apologia [i.e. the Augsburg Confession] in his kingdom, would, it seems to me, give much trouble to the papists
and disturb their plans for the council, provided that His
Royal Majesty is truly in earnest. Since all this has come
about without our seeking, it may well be so that God is
conducting things in a higher and better way than we can
comprehend. Now since he is about to give us friendly greet-
ing, it is clearly our obligation not to let him pass by without
thanks.'[114] Luther added that he approved of Melanchthon's
invitation to England. *He* was never much alarmed about the
concessions which Melanchthon might make, neither in 1530
at the time of the Augsburg Confession nor in 1536 when the
Wittenberg Articles were composed by Melanchthon on the
basis of the *Augustana* for discussion in England. Melanchthon knew well enough the extent of Luther's tolerance for
his conciliatory moves. He became a problem only after
Luther's death.

There cannot be any doubt that Melanchthon would have
liked to accept the invitations, and he reacted with some
bitterness to John Frederick's lack of confidence. The pros-
pect of the visit to England, however, was not yet fully ex-
plored when the news reached Wittenberg that Henry VIII
had had Fisher and More executed. The Lutherans were so
appalled that even Robert Barnes, their old friend, was received by them with great reserve. They had little reason to
revere the memory of Sir Thomas More and the Bishop of
Rochester, but despite all controversies they respected them
and, in any case, realized the significance of the beheading of
two men who had given such magnificent service to their
King. The horror of contemporaries, both of the old and of
the new religion, is testified by the multitude of translations

and reprints[115] of a Paris newsletter *A Reliable Report about
the Death of Thomas More* which says: 'those who are shed-
ding tears in mourning for Thomas More are not only his
former friends but even those who were bitterly opposed to
him. Enemies and friends have known him well. Never has
a scholar gone away from him without having been enriched;
whosoever had been with him was obliged to him for his
friendliness and kindness.'* Melanchthon hastened to write
an apology to Camerarius for having dedicated his *Loci
Communes* to Henry VIII.[116] In subsequent editions the dedi-
cation was omitted.

The reaction was the same elsewhere. In France, the King
lost even the sympathy of Cardinal du Bellay who now turned
against him at last. Special memoranda were drawn up in
England to explain the executions. The one composed for
French readers tried cleverly to represent Francis as sharing
the responsibility. Another, for Lutheran consumption, dealt
with a rumour supposed to be current in Germany that Fisher
and More had earned their fate because they had upheld the
evangelical doctrine against the King and persistently opposed the King's marriage with Anne Boleyn. To this the
writer replies that surely the erudite Germans would not
listen to such vulgar rumours since the King's benign disposi-
tion, his equity, piety and mildness were known throughout
the world.[117] The deed, however, spoke louder than the
memoranda.

Henry VIII, undisturbed, continued his attempts to persuade Melanchthon to come to England. He apparently never
realized when something had come to an end. As late as
October 1539 John Frederick had to oppose the invitation,
writing to Chancellor Brück: 'I cannot persuade myself to
like the idea of Philip Melanchthon's journey to England. The
King has gone to such lengths that Philip's life would be in

* According to Professor H. de Vocht of Louvain University, the Paris
newsletter (from which most of the translations derive) was probably based
on a report written by Erasmus and addressed to his friends, a report which
is no longer extant. Erasmus found himself even on such an occasion, once
again unable to take a clear stand, anxious not to make enemies and not to
risk financial loss. He wrote his report anonymously, pretending that it was
written in Paris by a young scholar to a friend, a native of Cologne. In order
to dispel any possible suspicion, he even wrote the remark that More's death
might soon be followed by that of Erasmus, providing the latter was still
alive (de Vocht, *Acta Thomae Mori* (1947), pp. 56 f. and 84).

danger if he spoke against his hazy, unchristian articles; or else, if he did not do so, he would have to flatter the King which we would not welcome.' [118]

4

At the time when Henry VIII was first trying to make Melanchthon come to England, he was also preparing for the greatest of the English missions to the League of Schmalkald. We have already quoted from a letter of Luther's in which he urged the Elector's chancellor to arrange for a friendly reception of Robert Barnes. Now it was the Elector who officially instructed the Wittenberg theologians to deal with the great delegation which Barnes had announced; nevertheless, he added the advice that no hasty decisions should be made. His letter, addressed to Luther, Melanchthon, Justus Jonas, Bugenhagen and Cruciger, begins:

'Our greetings, reverend, learned, beloved, pious and faithful sirs. As you know, the King of England recently had his orator Dr. Anthony Barnes here with us concerning certain inquiries. The doctor announced, among other things, that the king will send yet another formidable mission to converse with you, our theologians, about various articles and to have friendly talks and colloquies. It is our wish to let you know that you should receive the ambassadors and talk and confer with them. We should like you to receive them at Wittenberg, or on account of the plague at Wittenberg you may proceed, at our expense, to Torgau. It is our wish that you should listen to them with good will and that you should provide good answers. Whatever you may learn from them and whatever will be discussed, please report to us so that we shall be able to answer them easily. . . .' [119]

We have already mentioned that it was the primary aim of the mission to cause the Protestant princes to issue a formal petition to the King of England to join them. This part of the programme was very successful. Fox and Heath arrived at Erfurt, followed by an impressive train of servants and horses,

on November 28th, 1535. On December 9th they were received in audience by John Frederick at Weimar. From there
they proceeded together to Schmalkalden. On December 15th
Fox delivered a long speech in which he stressed the Protestant intentions of the King, asking for further opportunities
of discussing theological matters with the Lutherans in order
to create a common front for the council. The substance of
the speech harmonized with the hopes and expectations of
the princes, and on December 25th their petition was signed.
The most important point among the Lutheran conditions
was once again emphasized by John Frederick to the Bishop
of Hereford on December 25th: that the King would be expected to promote the Gospel and the Augsburg Confession
before a general council unless a few details were modified
by common consent. So much insistence on his obligations
was uncongenial to Henry VIII whose answer arrived in Wittenberg on March 12th, 1536: 'that he will and has long since
minded to set forth true and sincere doctrine; but, being a
king reckoned somewhat learned, though unworthy, and having also so many learned men in his realm, he cannot accept
at any creature's hand the observing of his and the realm's
faith, the ground whereof is in Scripture'.[120]

Such animosities did not influence the immediate negotiations because the talks at Schmalkalden were concerned with
the political and military issues, whereas the theological
points were to be discussed at Wittenberg afterwards. In the
case of a treaty Henry VIII would contribute 100,000 or 200,000
crowns to the League for defence purposes. The League
should provide Henry, were he attacked in a religious war or
on account of the League, with 500 horsemen or ten war-
ships and also, but this at Henry's expense, with an additional
2,000 horsemen and 5,000 warriors. This was more or less the
same proposal that Henry had offered to Lübeck and its allies.
These negotiations came to nothing because Henry's ambassadors also met the heralds of King Christian III of Denmark
at Schmalkalden. On December 23rd John Frederick of
Saxony and Philip of Hesse wrote to Henry that they were
resolved to assist Christian against Lübeck; they asked Henry
to join them in this matter, which, of course, was quite impossible for him.[121] Henry wanted the League exclusively as a
means of pressure, and possibly of defence, against Charles V.

The whole negotiations were complicated by certain fundamental misunderstandings on both sides. Henry VIII had
always regarded ecclesiastical affairs as subordinate to the
immediate aims of his personal, secular policy. It had been
almost accidental that the ecclesiastical policy which he had
finally adopted as an outcome of the matrimonial cause had
automatically created doctrinal conflicts which went far
beyond a redefinition of papal power in England. Henry VIII,
as we have stressed so frequently, had no desire to interfere
with doctrine; yet *nolens volens* he had to make doctrinal
adjustments. In the course of his experience he gradually
became accustomed to regard church affairs as even more
easily adjustable to the demands of momentary expediency than secular concerns. When he first began to contem-
plate joining the League, not simply as a member but as the
'Defender' of the Protestant League, he may have honestly
thought that he could become the 'leader' of the Lutherans
without becoming a Lutheran himself. It rarely occurred to
Henry VIII that other people's opinions were of importance.
Thus, when he found that the Lutherans took their religion
seriously, he was offended. His reply to John Frederick's
letter of December 25th—our last quotation—was perfectly
reasonable but for the crucial point that Henry wanted to
become the leader of the Lutherans, and they, though quite
aware of the learning of many English theologians, had little
cause for implicit trust in Henry's religious aims.

And thus the negotiations dragged on until 1540.

6

From Schmalkalden, the English ambassadors travelled to
Wittenberg where they arrived on January 1st. What was
intended to be a conference yielding quick, if preliminary,
results became an endless discussion which lasted for over
three months. Luther had little idea of how long the guests
would stay when, on January 25th, he wrote impatiently to
John Frederick: '... I had hoped we would finish with the
English ambassadors within three days, but they do not show
the slightest intention of leaving. I dare say, I have achieved

bigger things and more work in the course of four weeks, and they have now been quarrelling over this one point for twelve years. And they proceed in such a way that they will never come to results nor ever be able to give up.' As is indicated in this letter, Henry's ambassadors had once again opened the conversations about the divorce. In August of the previous year, Barnes had been supposed to make another effort but no opportunity had offered itself because, as Barnes had written to Cromwell on August 22nd: '... the whole university has left Wittenberg for the fear of the plague, so that I can do no good yet, for no one is here but Martin'.[122]

The English theologians were, as can be imagined, quite extravagantly knowledgeable on the subject of matrimonial law, and they proved to the Lutherans that the prohibition in Mosaic law against marriage with a deceased brother's wife belonged to natural law and referred to the wife of a brother either living or deceased. The Lutherans admitted their mistake, but they could not give their approval to the dissolution of a marriage once it had been contracted. This part of the conference was at long last terminated in March. The Lutherans wrote a revised version of their verdict which, for that matter, was in effect no different from the previous one: they disapproved of the divorce.

Two months before this, on January 11th, Luther had written to the Elector, reporting to him that he had heard that an official verdict concerning the status of Catherine and Anne Boleyn was to be announced by all the judges of the English realm. 'I will not make a serious study of their games with jurisprudence and I could not do more than reply: "gaag" like a goose. I suppose I shall stand by my previous decision, but otherwise I shall not be unobliging to them in this or that detail; they must not think that we Germans are made of stone or wood. Only, I refrain from talking about it over the table as otherwise all the stable boys would discuss the cause in the streets.' [123]

The discussions of the divorce were carried on despite Catherine's death on January 9th, 1536; their chief point was, as it always had been, the settlement of the succession. On January 19th, Luther wrote to Caspar Müller, Chancellor of the Dukes of Mansfeld: '... I have nothing specially to report about the English deputation. How curious you Mans-

felders are! The queen is dead. One hears that also the young
lady, the daughter, is seriously ill. But she has lost her cause
in all the world except with us poor beggars, the theologians
at Wittenberg, who would have liked to preserve her royal
honours had she lived. That's now the end of that. The Pope
has acted in this affair truly as a pope, issuing contradictory
Bulls. The way he has played the game it serves him right
that he has been thrown out of England—even if it did not
happen in the cause of the Gospel. He has tossed about the
King in such a fashion that I feel almost inclined to excuse the
King personally; and yet I cannot consent to his cause. . . .'[124]

A private letter like this shows more clearly than the
cautious hairsplitting discussions about the subtleties of the
Mosaic law that Luther was firmly persuaded in the matter.
While in England Anne Boleyn was considered to be the
chief champion of a movement in sympathy with Lutheranism, the Lutherans' sympathy was entirely on the side of
Catherine of Aragon and her daughter Mary. One can easily
imagine that this went beyond the comprehension of Henry
VIII. And it was by no means Luther alone who held such
opinions. When the shattering news of Anne Boleyn's execution reached the astonished Lutherans, John Frederick wrote
to Duke Wilhelm of Neuenahr that he and all his circle had
never approved of the King's marriage 'with his former
mistress whom he has now ordered to be killed'.[125]

7

Infinitely more complicated than the endless arguments about
the divorce were the theological discussions. The English
concentrated chiefly on three points in which they demanded
concessions from the Lutherans: communion under one kind,
the private Mass and the celibacy of priests. The Lutherans
were, first of all, concerned with basic doctrine.

Luther had the idea of demonstrating the Lutheran stand-
point to his visitors by means of a *disputatio extraordinaria* in
the university. He wrote the theses and Melanchthon composed the counter-arguments. Thus, the Lutherans demonstrated on January 14th their teaching regarding justification

and on January 29th that on the private Mass. Those taking
part were Luther, Melanchthon, Bugenhagen, Cruciger, Jonas,
Weller and Burchard; it is not known whether the English
theologians actively participated in the disputations.

The progress, such as it was, of the conversations culmi-
nated in Melanchthon's composition of the so-called *Wittenberg Articles* of 1536, which are largely extracts from the
Augsburg Confession and its *Apologia*. They produced in
England the reaction of the *Ten Articles* of June 11th, 1536,
which were a masterpiece of evasion. In particular, there is
no mention of the Mass and thus the central point of the
controversy between the old and the new teaching remains
obscure. On the other hand, indulgences and Masses for the
departed are denounced as abuses. Perhaps one may say that
the Ten Articles represent the maximum of concession Henry
VIII was prepared to grant to the Lutherans, for reasons, to
be sure, other than personal conviction.

Anyway, by the time that the *Wittenberg Articles* were
drawn up, Luther was no longer much concerned with the
English affairs which he had delegated to Melanchthon. Long
before the departure of the ambassadors, he wrote to Burchard, that he was 'thoroughly sick of this kind of disputation,
if, indeed, one can use this term for such quarrels'. It was, he
wrote, the sort of thing well known to him through Zwingli
and Carlstadt, and it led nowhere.

But Luther intervened once again when at long last the
English theologians were willing to show the *Wittenberg
Articles* to Henry VIII as a basis for future discussions which
were to be held in England. On March 28th, 1536, Luther
wrote to John Frederick: '. . . If now his royal Majesty should
accept the articles then the treaty can be further discussed.
The articles do rhyme with our teaching. Whenever they
wish it, a mission can be sent over to give further explanations to the King. However, if his royal Majesty will not accept these articles, or demand a lot of alterations, then I say:
we truly cannot upset our church once again for his sake,
considering that it has only just achieved tranquillity.' To
Nicolas Hausmann, Luther wrote: 'The English deputation
to Magister Philip [Melanchthon] awaits the success of the
King's efforts. But I have to concern myself with many things
and cannot therefore follow everything in detail.'[126]

Much as Luther wished to leave the affair entirely to Melanchthon, he had to consider yet another formal inquiry from the castle as to whether further concessions could be granted. He replied on April 20th to the effect that he could not make concessions to the King of England which he had refused to the Pope:

'. . . It is quite true that one must be patient because one cannot expect a sudden doctrinal settlement in England (with us, too, it was a slow process). But the main articles cannot be altered or left out. Ceremonial things are temporal affairs and will be dealt with in good time under reasonable sovereigns; there is no need to quarrel or to worry much about them provided the basis is sound.

'The question whether or not the treaty with the King ought to be made, should the latter fail to agree with all the articles, I will leave to the decision of the princes and of my gracious lord, it being a worldly thing. I consider it dangerous to make a treaty if the hearts are not of one mind. . . .'[127]

8

If Luther had little to do with the conferences of 1536 at Wittenberg, he was even less involved with the continuation of the discussions.

The Ten Articles of 1536 had mentioned only three sacraments, keeping a discreet silence about the other four which were under dispute. Doubts about the right interpretation of the omission were removed by the publication, in 1537, of the *Godly and Pious Institution of Christian Man*; this made mention of all seven sacraments. It was one of those moments when the Lutheran alliance was not so important.

The meeting of Charles V and Francis at Aigues Mortes and their conferences with Pope Paul III, however, lead to renewed contacts with the Lutherans, early in the year 1538. On February 25th Henry VIII wrote to John Frederick of Saxony and to Philip of Hesse that he was sending over Christopher Mont to discuss religion with them and that he desired the promised Lutheran mission to England to be dispatched soon.[128] On February 28th instructions were issued to Mont. He was to find out whether the League of Protestant Princes concerned itself solely with religious treaties or whether there was any possibility of making a purely political treaty. This shows yet once again how stubbornly Henry VIII could maintain his schemes even when they had been quite definitely rejected. Mont was also instructed to insist that Melanchthon should be among the Lutheran delegation. Melanchthon, it seems, had a firmly established reputation in England for being either a weakling or a sympathizer with Henry's reformation. The English negotiators invariably set high hopes on Melanchthon's conciliatory nature.[129] It was a mistaken estimation of Melanchthon's true attitude. In fact, he had summarized his impression of the Ten Articles by calling them *confussissime compositi*.[130] And on the margin of another English document he had written, in Greek, 'nothing sound'.

Mont was further instructed: 'If anyone speak of the king's supremacy, he shall say that at the coming of their embassy they shall be fully satisfied therein; for his *own* opinion he shall cite such scriptures as are contained in a letter written by the bishops of London and Durham.'[131]

The preliminary negotiations concerning the planned embassy to England went on for a while. The problem of keeping Melanchthon out without giving offence to Henry VIII was disposed of with the argument that some of the learned Lutherans had to stay behind because they might be needed to take part in the council at Vicenza. In any case, the answer to Henry stated, Mont had failed to make clear Henry's attitude to the Lutheran doctrines; consequently, it would be the primary task of the embassy to hear Henry declare his views.[132] Melanchthon wrote a suitably flattering letter to Henry, playing on the King's favourite compliment ('excelling others so much in learning and wisdom') and recommending Burchard to him.[133]

At long last the Lutheran delegation was dispatched and arrived in London on May 31st; it consisted of Franz Burchard, the Hesse councillor George of Boyneburg and Frederick Myconius. They brought with them from Luther a friendly, personal letter to Bishop Fox.

'Grace and peace in Christ, our Lord. As now our good friends and messengers make themselves ready for the journey to your illustrious king, I feel I must write a letter to you lest otherwise I might be regarded as an ungrateful, forgetful man. Quite apart from the great pleasure of your company which we here enjoyed so much, I remember your great kindness, the advice you gave me concerning my opponent Calculus. How then could I ever forget you? We often spoke of you, particularly since the great change in your kingdom either makes it impossible for you to write to us, or else letters are perhaps intercepted; such are the explanations with which we comfort ourselves. For we began to be in doubt, almost in fear, that the persistent silence might possibly imply that the progress of the Gospel had met a sad hindrance. We even heard rumours that your king, deceived by popish snares, was trying to obtain a reconciliation with the Pope. Here we pray and wish between fear and hope that Satan may be caught beneath your foot. We know nothing with any degree of certainty how things stand with you regarding the Gospel. We only hope that on their return, our messengers will bring with them glad tidings, truly evangelical tidings, from your English church. As regards church and secular affairs in our Germany, you can obtain full and ample news from our friends. May the Lord Jesus Christ increase His gifts and His grace in both you and us, to the honour of the Father. Amen. My Kathi sends her reverent greetings. Farewell in Christ and allow me to recommend myself to you.

12 May 1538   yours Martin Luther.'[134]

The Lutheran delegation stayed right through the summer. There is no need here to describe the pitifully slow progress of the consultations in which the Germans tried to make the English commit themselves in one way or another—precisely what Henry wished to avoid in any circumstances. By August 18th the Lutherans had lost patience and were only with difficulty persuaded by Cranmer to stay another week; finally, they agreed to wait another month.[135]

On August 23rd Cranmer wrote to Cromwell that the trouble was that the bishops did not dare to give a written statement to the Germans because they were uncertain how

the King wished to answer them. They were—the usual pre-
dicament of Henry VIII's trusted executives—afraid of writing anything contrary to the King's wishes. Cranmer added
that the Germans had an additional reason to be in a hurry.
They were badly lodged; rats ran about in their chambers
and the kitchen was too close to the parlour.[136]

In the end they were given one of those noncommittal
answers which left all essentials open, and when they returned home Henry wrote a courteous letter to John
Frederick, informing him benevolently that the embassy had
given evidence of sound erudition and Christian piety and
that he felt assured in his hopes for eventual good results.
Finally, he recommended once again that Melanchthon
should come to England to conclude the matter.[137]

Earlier in that year it really should at last have become
clear to Henry that Melanchthon's visit would be of no use to
him. On March 26th Melanchthon had written to him that
he was still desirous that 'a union *upon the basis of doctrinal
agreement* should be effected among those churches which
reject the domination of Rome'.[138] The King had probably
overlooked the hint.

The results, then, of the German embassy had been nil.
Henry VIII had throughout entertained the very same hope
which had first caused him to seek an alliance with the
Lutheran princes: that they would accept him without satisfaction of their religious demands. In a conference with the
Lutheran theologians he explained 'that he was willing to
enter into a league ... and *afterwards* he would treat with
them about entering into a league of religion'.[139] As we have
seen all along, this was precisely what the Lutherans resolved
to prevent: to admit Henry into the League without being
certain about his religious intentions.

The only tangible outcome of all the negotiations were the
Thirteen Articles of 1538. They agree in their arrangement
and frequently in their contents and wording with the Augsburg Confession. Certain articles were deliberately expressed
without clarity, for instance those concerned with justification and Holy Communion. In any case these Articles remained inconsequential for the immediate future as Henry
VIII would not approve of them, but they form the basis for
the *Forty-two Articles* of 1553.

During the later part of 1538 and the beginning of the next year, the relationship between Charles V and Francis I determined Henry's quite amazing vacillations. Whenever news was received of disagreement among them, he adopted the part (which, no doubt, he liked best) of the virtuous Catholic prince, and when the news reported the threat of harmony between them, he made a fresh move in his approaches to the Lutherans. Thus in April 1539 a further deputation of Lutherans arrived in London, invited by the King. This time, however, there were no interminable negotiations. In May the King learned to his disgust that the Lutheran princes had made a peace settlement with Charles, a move which made Lutheranism quite unattractive as far as he was concerned. Promptly, on May 16th, the *Six Articles* Act was published ('An Act abolishing Diversity in Opinion') which made all further contact with the Lutherans impossible.

A few months later, on July 10th, the table talk touched on Henry VIII, and Luther reacted with the exclamation that he thanked God 'for having delivered us from this exasperating King of England who has so eagerly sought a treaty with our princes and yet could not be accepted. No doubt, God prevented it by his special counsel, for he has always been inconsistent and uncertain. He wants to be the head of the Church in England immediately after Christ, a title for which no bishop, however pious and blessed, is fit, not to mention a king or a prince. It is insufferable. Christ alone is the bridegroom and head of His Christian Church. The Church is not as lowly a body as the Pope seems to dream. However, the devil sits astride on this king so that he vexes and plagues Christ. He has killed Thomas More, who has sinned against God, but who has not done anything against the king. He is and remains King Harry but it won't be long and he will come to grief. It is a great pity that magister Philippus has addressed some of his most beautiful prefaces to the worst people.'

The Six Articles can probably be regarded as reflecting Henry's religious mind. They were issued at a time when his reformation had provided everything that he had wished to gain by it. The power of the papacy in England had vanished; the matrimonial affair had ended in a tolerable, if not perfect solution; between 1536 and 1539 the dissolution of the monasteries had been effected. As soon as the Act for the Dissolution of the Greater Monasteries had vested all monastic property summarily in the King, the Six Articles restored traditional Catholic conceptions which had been the subject-matter of the four years' discussions with the Lutherans. That minor problem, Henry's latest marriage to Anne of Cleves, had been settled in the King's mind ever since he first set eyes on her and was not regarded by him as a real obstacle. The disgust she inspired in him was quite possibly making Lutherans in general even less likeable to the King, and he certainly revised very rapidly his opinion of Robert Barnes, who had procured the latest bride. From any point of view whatever, Protestantism had yielded what it was worth to Henry: power and money. Whatever doctrinal changes were made served the sole purpose of demonstrating that power and money had been obtained, not unlike the divorce from Catherine, in obedience to God's Word and the King's delicate conscience.

The publication of the Six Articles was followed by a period of reorientation of Henry's foreign policy and of his status at home. By the beginning of 1540 the experimental stage of careful exploration was over. In April Cromwell was created Earl of Essex, in June he was sent to the Tower and on July 28th he was beheaded. When Convocation decided on July 7th that the King's marriage with Anne of Cleves was 'null and void' the lady did nothing to obstruct the decision: she survived.

It is difficult to say whether or not the Six Articles represent the religious views of the majority of the English at the time. The threats of punishment which have so prominent a place seem to suggest an unpopular Act. Of the twenty-seven executions for heresy between 1534 and 1547, twenty-one took place after the Six Articles Act.[140] However that may be, the concept of popularity hardly ever troubled Henry VIII except in times when the results of his policy led to a threat of general insurrection. Naturally, the wishes of his subjects were always very close to his heart. Had he not applied for the divorce from Catherine of Aragon because the common people had demanded it? Had he not married Anne Boleyn in obedience to the same irresistible *vox Dei*? The fact that the Six Articles were issued after four years of searching discussions with the Lutherans does not in any way reveal what 'the people' wanted. It only proves what Henry wanted.

We are not here discussing the theological substance of Henry VIII's experimental phases of Protestantism and traditionalism. There are, to be sure, purer sources available for the comparative study of Catholic and Lutheran doctrine than the state papers of Henry VIII. We are only concerned with the impact of these articles on the relations between the King and the Lutherans. There was hardly anybody left with illusions; but Martin Bucer took it upon himself to write to John Frederick of Saxony and to Luther, urging them to make one further approach to the King of England.

Luther was convinced that this was unnecessary and a paragraph in his letter to Bucer of October 14th says: 'Regarding the King of England, I fear you will see your hopes deceived. The English who have stayed with us have themselves often complained about their king and have envied us our liberty. Quite recently, an ambassador visited our prince, but he neither brought anything with him nor did he take anything away with him that could give us some hope. May the Lord direct his heart and the heart of all other kings to His glory.'[141]

On October 23rd, Luther, Melanchthon, Bugenhagen and Jonas stated their views to John Frederick: '... Although we ourselves do not avoid dangerous and troublesome tasks, it is surely right to say that enough has been done in this matter to serve the king with instruction and admonition. Saint Paul says that we should assist those who are weak but we should let the stiff-necked go his own way, for he is condemned by his own judgment; that is, if he acts openly against his own conscience. To express it differently, a man is called *weak* who is eager to learn, does not combat against what he has comprehended but accepts it, holds on to it and follows it. It is obvious that the King of England acts against his conscience. He knows that our doctrine and practice relating to the whole sacrament, to penance and to the marriage of priests is right; or, at least he knows that our teaching does not stand in contradiction with the Word of God. Now he says in his articles and in the *edictum* that some of these points were against God's law. This he certainly maintains against his own conscience because many writings which he

has studied were especially written for him. He has had
enough reports, both from ourselves and through his emis-
saries. He himself has caused a book of Sarcerius to be translated into his own language and ordered it to be printed; he
is using it for his prayer book and in it these points are dealt
with concisely. We have also heard that he has talked much
about his doctrine and, referring to France, he has remarked
that all who oppose his doctrine are wicked because he had
the right understanding of such things. He also has many
devout and well instructed divines (the dismissed Bishop
Latimer, Cranmer and others) to whom he has listened and
whom he has tolerated for a while. Now he goes against all
this, condemns this doctrine more violently than the Pope
(who has never said that the marriage of priests is against
God's law, that it is God's commandment to enumerate sins
in confession). Otherwise he punishes like Nebugdonosur and
the pillar, wishing to kill off anyone who does not agree with
those articles. He has indeed begun a dreadful persecution
and there are many in prison waiting for their punishment.
He has used this doctrine for a time for his own purpose, like
Herod, but now he persecutes it and Satan begins another
crafty strife. . . . He prefers to make his own religion, as Anti-
ochus and others have done. . . .

'Further, since the King is acting against his own conscience we do not consider ourselves obliged to instruct him
yet again. We will follow Saint Paul's rule which teaches us
to admonish our adversaries twice; if that does not help, one
should avoid them for they act against their true conscience.
Such admonitions have been given and yet he rails against
his conscience; instruction is lost on such people.

'We also hear that the King is a glossator, colouring everything with glosses and with illusions. He who has no love for
the clear truth can turn and twist himself although thereby
he may rend his mouth like the fish trying to escape from
the hook. . . . Since the King takes pleasure in making such
glosses, we have little hope that he will listen to instruction
and surrender to God's word.

'See, too, what sort of people now have power under him;
they, too, have no conscience. Wintoniensis travels about

with two unchaste women in men's attire; that is the premiss from which he concludes that the marriage of priests is against God's law. And he is so proud that he said openly, he would uphold against the whole world that the proposition *fide justificamur* is wrong. He is also the most dreadful tyrant who has burned two people only because of the transsubstantiation. One does see here that the proverb is true which says "Like servant, like master".

'From all this we conclude that enough has been done. We know with certainty that we are not obliged to carry on with him. It would be a hopeless enterprise and it may well be so that God does not want His Gospel dishonoured by this king who has so evil a reputation. However, we leave your Grace to decide whether we should try once again. We will not fail to write, all of us together, an expostulation to the King, to admonish him once again in writing; more we cannot do. . . .'[142]

On the same day, Luther wrote a private letter to John Frederick in which he made it quite clear that the common memorandum had his full approval.

'. . . I have replied to Bucer that he should give up all hope because it is no use with the King. It is therefore my humble petition that your Grace maintain the opinion reached. The King is a tempter and means nothing sincerely. This we have learned well enough through the English who have been here with us at a time when we had to believe, in charity, that their concern was serious; but at long last, when we had disputed to the point of exhaustion, at the expense of your Grace, the whole thing was dropped then and there, for it depended on the King's whims. They said themselves: *Rex noster est inconstans.* And Dr. Antonius said repeatedly: our King does not altogether care for religion and for the Gospel. Since that time I am glad that at long last the King has caused an open breach, that he has revealed his duplicity. It would never have been well to make common cause with him; we would have loaded ourselves with his sins and even then he would have been a false friend. Not to mention that the English visitors made it known to us that we would have been required to let the King be and call himself *caput* of the English Church. Good riddance, Head and Defender! Gold and money makes him so frivolous that he thinks he is worthy of adoration and that God could no longer manage without him. May he himself carry his unrepented sins; we have enough with our own. We have done more than what was necessary. His behaviour towards the Emperor Maximilian and soon afterwards towards King Louis of France, has been the same. Let him then be a pope, as truly he is in England. May our Lord God protect your Grace and all your family from all evil and particularly from such crafty, clever schemes of the devil, Amen.'[143]

Part V

EPILOGUE

Two days after Cromwell's execution, on July 30th 1540, six men were burned at Smithfield, three of them for heresy, the other three for denying the King's supremacy, i.e., for treason. Among the 'heretics' of the day was Dr. Robert Barnes who had been Henry VIII's chief instrument during many years of approaches to Luther. He may well have been, as Dr. Gairdner emphasized, 'arrogant, dogmatic, and conceited far beyond what his real attainments justified'; but had he not, as Luther said of Saint Thomas More, served his king well?

According to a contemporary broadsheet, debates about Henry VIII's reformation continued elsewhere. It tells of the 'Metynge of Doctor Barnes and Doctor Powell at Paradise Gate and of theyr coomunicacion both drawen to Smyth-fylde from the Tower. The one burned for Heresye as the papistes saye truly and the other quartered for popery and all within one houre.' At Paradise Gate, Dr. Powell had the last word, promising further tribulation, to his fellow-martyr:

> Thou saist thou comest to have rest.
> Thou shalt be the deuels geste
> And herto I wyll do my best
> Thou mayst be sure therfore.

The copy of the broadsheet in the British Museum suggests that the debate also continued on earth: the word 'truly' in the title has been changed to 'untruly' by a contemporary hand.

Elsewhere, a different epitaph was written in memory of the one person who had known both Henry VIII and Martin Luther and who had yet considered that religious concord between them was not impossible. In the year of Barnes's

death, his *Articles of Faith* were published at Wittenberg and
Luther wrote this preface:

'This doctor Barnes who in exceptional humility refused to
be addressed as a doctor called himself Antonius. This was
indeed his right since he was formerly imprisoned by the
Holy Bishops of the Holy Papists and only released with
great difficulty. And I say, we knew him well, this doctor.
Now, it is indeed a wondrous joy to learn that our good, pious
brother and table companion and member of our household
has been permitted by God's grace to shed his blood for the
sake of His beloved Son and to become a holy martyr. Thanks,
praise and honour be unto the Father of our beloved Lord
Jesus Christ who has shown us again this time, as in the beginning, how His Christians are being removed from our
sight and presence to suffer pain, i.e., how those attain
Heaven and become saints who have eaten and drunk with
us (as the apostles say of Christ, Acts iv) and who have joined
in our gaiety. Who would have believed twenty years ago
that our Lord Christ was so near unto us and eaten, drunk,
conversed and lived with us at our table in our very house
through his dear martyr and beloved saint. How grave and
desolate has been that evil, accursed papacy; it has never left
us a saint on earth. But he calls himself "the Most Holy"
and has heaped up before us saints of his own choice although
he knew quite well that there was as little truth in it as if the
devil were called "the Most Holy". But nothing further about
this just now.
'There was a time when this holy martyr Sanct Robertus
learned that his King (begging his pardon) Harry of England
had become hostile to the Pope and he went back to England
in the hope there to plant the Gospel, in his fatherland. At
last he also achieved a beginning. In short, Harry of England
treated him according to his own fashion until he sent him to
us at Wittenberg in connection with the matrimonial question; about this, something like thirty-three universities had
given what they called judgments and all of them had told
Harry that he should send away his Queen, Frau Katherin,
the aunt of Emperor Charles, and to take another (as he had
anyhow done).
'But when we had conversed for a long time at the con-

siderable expense of our gracious lord, the Elector of Saxony, we found out in the end that Harry of England had not at all sent over his ambassadors because he wanted to accept the Gospel, but only so that we at Wittenberg should approve of his *repudium* or divorce. I became quite angry that I, together with our theologians, had given so much work to this religious inquiry of theirs. And when we had reached certain results, they said that their King would not like the four articles, to do away with celibacy, the Mass and monasticism, to allow Holy Communion in both kinds. "Yes," I said, "we have been led up the garden path; they might have told us that before. Your king takes away the Pope's money and retains his kind of government." Thus, Harry is pope in England and the Pope is Harry in England.

'He himself, Dr. Robert Barnes, told me often enough: "*Rex noster non curat religionum, sed est*" and so forth. But so great was his love for his King and country that he bore all this willingly; he always wished to help England. This is assuredly true. A man is indeed worthy of contempt who does not love his own country and wish his prince well, as we know not only through Scripture but also through the law. That is why he always had this word on his lips: *Rex meus, regem meum*. And his confession testifies that he has been faithful and loving to the *Rex meum* to the very hour of his death; but from Harry he got an evil reward for it. He was deceived by hope. Always he hoped that at long last his King would become a good man.

'Among other things, we often discussed why the King desires to use the disgusting title *Defensor Fidei et in terris caput supremum et immediatum post Christum Ecclesiae Anglicanae*. What answer we got amounted to "*Sic volo, sic iubeo, sit pratione voluntas*". This in order to show once again that Harry wants to be God and do what he likes.

'One thing is still unknown: the reason for which he was martyred. Because Harry is ashamed of it. But it may well be so as many honest people have said, namely that Doctor Barnes (like Saint John the Baptist against Herod) spoke up against Harry and would not consent that he had thrown off the lady from Julich and taken another woman. For, whatever Harry wants that must be regarded as an article of faith both for life and death. Doctor Barnes told me himself that

More and the Bishop of Rochester had been executed by
Harry because they would not consent to articles made by
him.

'As to Harry: we will let him depart to all his Harries with
all his Harries where they belong. We should give thanks to
God, the Father of mercy, that He can make such masterly
use of such devils and devil's companions towards our and all
Christians' salvation and also to the punishment of themselves
and of all who do not wish to know God; as He has always
done through dreadful tyrants. As Saint Paul says, Romans
VIII, all things must work for good, all that exists, is done
and suffered; all to the peril of those who persecute God's
children. Likewise it is with our robber Harry: by doing evil
he achieves so much good that I think, even if he were in
Paradise he would suffer all pains of hell through his anger
that things did not happen as he wanted them. About this
more another time and better expressed. Let us praise and
thank God. This is a blessed time for the chosen saints of
Christ and an accursed, evil time for the devil, the blas-
phemers and adversaries. And it shall become worse. Amen.'

It would be desirable, in fairness to Henry VIII, to quote
what he had to say about Martin Luther when the relations
between them had come to an end. Perhaps he said as little
about him as about Saint Thomas More, the Queens Catherine and Anne Boleyn, Cardinal Wolsey, and many others,
once these persons had ceased, some of them not altogether
accidentally, to cross his path.

REFERENCES AND NOTES

1. Ch. Sturge, *Cuthbert Tunstall* (1938), p. 361 f.
2. *Letters and Papers*, III, 1233.
3. *Letters and Papers*, III, 1247.
4. R. H. Murray, *Erasmus and Luther* (1920), p. 179 f.; J. Huizinga, *Erasmus of Roterdam*, transl. F. Hopman (1952), p. 142 f.; E. M. G. Routh, *Sir Thomas More and his Friends* (1934), pp. 100 and 189 f.
5. *Des. Erasmi Roterodami Opus Epistolarum* (ed. Allen, 1906 etc.) VII, 1878.
6. Ch. Sturge, *op. cit.*, p. 361 f.
7. *Letters and Papers*, III, 1210.
8. H. Ellis, *Original Letters illustrative of English History*, Third Series, I (1846), p. 239 f.
9. Strype, *Eccl. Memorials*, I, 1, p. 56; the complete text of the commission: I, 2, p. 20 f.
10. M. Brosch, *Geschichte von England* (1890), IV, p. 135
11. J. Gairdner, *The English Church in the Sixteenth Century* (1903), p. 89.
12. A copy of the newsletter is preserved in the British Museum, bound in a folio volume together with various odds and ends. (Cat. No. C.18.e.l.).
13. Burnet, *History of the Reformation* (1679), Part I, Records, p. 8; Wilkinson, *Concilia* (1737), III, p. 711; Ch. Sturge, *op. cit.*, p. 362 f.
14. P. Hughes, *The Reformation in England* (4th ed., 1956), I, p. 145.
15. A. W. Reed, *The Regulation of the Book Trade before the Royal Proclamation of 1538* (Transactions of the Bibliographical Society, XI, p. 214 f.).
16. *ibid.*, p. 170 f.
17. *Calendar of State Papers Henry VIII*, IV, 6402.
18. Strype, *op. cit.*, I, 1, p. 254; Wilkinson, *op. cit.*, III, 707.
19. For a list of all English books prohibited by name during the reign of Henry VIII, *vide* R. Steele, *Notes on English Books printed abroad 1525–48* (Transactions of the Bibliographical Society, XI, p. 214 f.).
20. F. S. Siebert, *Freedom of the Press in England 1476–1776* (1952), p. 44.
21. *loc. cit.*
22, F. H. Reusch, *Der Index der verbotenen Bücher* (1883) I, p. 98f.
23. A. F. Pollard, *Wolsey* (1929), p. 26.

24. *Calendar of State Papers, Venetian*, III, 796.

25. *Letters and Papers*, III, 1297.

26. From a draft corrected by Ruthall and Wolsey: *Letters and Papers*, III, 1510.

27. *Venetian State Papers*, III, 159.

28. H. Ellis, *op. cit.*, Third Series, I, p. 264.

29. *loc. cit.*

30. *Letters and Papers*, III, 1656.

31. H. Ellis, *op. cit.*, p. 266.

32. *Letters and Papers*, III, 1656.

33. Extracts from the Acta Consistorialia relating to the title in Creighton's *History of the Papacy* (1894), V, p. 321 f.

34. H. Ellis, *op. cit.*, p. 288.

35. E. Hall, *Henry VIII* (ed. Ch. Whibley, 1904), I, p. 235.

36. J. M. Brown, *Henry VIII's Book Assertio Septem Sacramentorum and the Royal Title.* . . . (Royal Historical Society's Transactions, VIII, p. 242 f.).

37. Foxe, *Actes and Monuments* (ed. J. Pratt), IV, p. 294 n.

38. Burnett, *op. cit.*, I, p. 68 f.

39. *Letters and Papers*, III, p. ccccxxvii.

40. P. Hughes, *op. cit.*, I, p. 147.

41. Foxe, *op. cit.*, p. 293.

42. Burnet, *op. cit.*, I, p. 68 n. Elsewhere he refers to the King as the author of the book.

43. J. M. Brown, *op. cit.*, p. 250 f.

44. *Letters and Papers*, III, 1273.

45. G. Rupp, *Studies in the Making of the English Protestant Tradition* (1947), p. 90.

46. W. Roper's *Lyfe of Sir Thomas More* (Early English Text Society ed., 1935), p. 66.

47. *Schutz vnd Handthabung der Sibben Sacrament wider Martinum Luter vo[n] dem aller vnuberwintlichsten König zu Engellandt vn Franckreych, vn hern in Hibernia, hern Heinriche dem achten dhis nhames ausgangenn.*

48. H. Ellis, *op. cit.*, p. 269 f.

49. Luther, *Briefe* (ed. de Wette), vol. I.

50. *Eruditissimi viri G. Rossi opus, quo refellit Lutheri calumnias quibus Angliae regi Henrico VIII insectatur.* Or, in the edition of More's Latin works of 1565, *Vindicatio Henrici VIII a calumniis Lutheri.*

51. Erasmus, *Opera* (1703), X, 1652. Mentioned by P. Smith in the English Historical Review, vol. XXV.

52. *Ob der künig usz engellandt oder der Luter eyn lügner sey.* The rare tract has been reprinted in J. Scheibel, *Das Kloster weltlich und geistlich* (1846), vol. IV.

53. *Letters and Papers*, III, 3029.

54. *The Correspondence of Sir Thomas More* (ed. E. F. Rogers), 1947, p. 276 f.

55. *Antwurt de Murnar uff seine frag ob der künig vo[n] Engellant ein liogner sey oder der götlich doctor Martinus Luter.*

56. P. Scherrer, *Zwei neue Schriften Thomas Murners* (Baseler Zeitschrift für Geschichte und Altertum, vol. XXIX, p. 146 f.). The entire text was afterwards published by Dr. Scherrer in the *Archiv für Elsässische Kirchengeschichte.*

57. Luther, *Werke* (ed. Walch), vol. XIX, col. 156.

58. Strype, *op. cit.*, I, 1, p. 64.

59. E. Wuelcker, *Des Kursächsischen Rathes Hans v.d. Planitz Berichte aus dem Reichsregiment in Nürnberg 1521–1523* (ed. H. Virck, 1899), p. 423 f.

60. *loc. cit.*, p. 429.

61. C. E. Forstemann, *Neues Urkundenbuch zur Geschichte der evangelischen Kirchenreform* (1842), I, p. 25.

62. Henry VIII's letter to the Saxonian princes is summarized in *Letters and Papers*, IV, 40. Frederick's reply is somewhat drastically abbreviated (*loc. cit.*, IV, 301); the argument is represented quite adequately but no hint is given of the admonitory dignity of its style.

63. For details of Christian II's career down to 1523 *vide* E. H. Dunkley, *The Reformation in Denmark* (1948), ch. I.

64. *Letters and Papers*, IV, 2371 and 3261.

65. *Letters and Papers*, IV, 2420.

66. *Correspondence of Sir Thomas More*, *op. cit.*, p. 368.

67. *Auff des königs zu engellandt lesterschrifft titel.*

68. *Fünff Vorredde des Hochwirdigen Vatters vnd Herren, H. Johann, Bischoffs von Roffa in Engellandt, uff V bücher wider Jo. Ecolompadium . . .*

69. *Underricht vnd gegeantwurt Doctor Johann Fabri, über die zornige vnd lesterschrifft Martini Luthers von wegen widerruffs des sich Lthtr [sic] gegen den Durchleutigisten Künig von Engellant erbotten hatt.*

70. Book Dedications of Cochlaeus: *Adversus latrocinantes* (1525) to Bishop Fisher; *Ruperti Abbatis . . . commentar. in Apocr. Johan.* (1526) to Henry VIII; the same, *in Matthaeum* (1526) to Bishop Fisher and the Archbishop of Capua; *Cassiodori Patr. Romani Consulum Romanorum Catalogus* (1528) to Sir Thomas More; *Ruperti Abbatis . . . de Victoria Verbi Dei* (1529) to Bishop West; *Dialogus de bello contra Turcos in antologias Lutheri, XV contradictiones* (1529) to Bishop Tunstall (here Luther is exposed as a secret ally of the Turks!); *Autenticae Justiniani Imp. Aug. de rebus sacris* (1529) to Bishop West; *Fasciculus calumniarum, sannarum . . . Lutheri* (1529) to Bishop Fisher.

71. Roper, *op. cit.*, p. 67 f.

72. The dispensation of Julius II to Henry VIII is quoted in N. Pocock, *Records of the Reformation* (1870), I, 1, p. 5.

K

73. Reported to Rome by Sanuto on Sept. 1st, 1514. *Venetian State Papers*, II, 188.
74. G. Mattingly, *Catherine of Aragon* (1942), p. 127.
75. W. Moeller, *Lehrbuch der Kirchengeschichte* (1907), vol. III, p. 202 f.
76. *Letters and Papers*, IV, 3802, 4120, 5072, 6290.
77. Rockwell, *op. cit.*, p. 295.
78. J. Gairdner, *Lollardy and the Reformation*, vol. I, p. 295.
79. *Spanish State Papers*, IV, 224.
80. J. Collier, *An Ecclesiastical History of Great Britain* (ed. Th. Lathbury, 1852), vol. IV, p. 147 f.
81. Pocock, *Documents . . .* , *op. cit.*, contains examples.
82. *Dictionary of National Biography*, vol. XIII, p. 120 f.
83. *Letters and Papers*, IV, 6149, 6229. Many of Cooke's reports are extensively quoted in Pocock's *Documents of the Reformation*.
84. *Letters and Papers*, IV, 6581.
85. *Letters and Papers*, IV, 1611.
86. *Letters and Papers*, V, 326.
87. Rockwell, *op. cit.*, p. 294 f.
88. *Letters and Papers*, IV, 6290.
89. Quoted by P. Smith, *English Historical Review*, vol. XXVII, p. 673.
90. P. Friedmann, *Anne Boleyn* (1884), I, pp. 157, 173, 187, 222.
91. *Spanish State Papers*, II, 379.
92. *Letters and Papers*, II, p. xxxiv n.; IV, 5859.
93. *Letters and Papers*, IV, 3422.
94. Luther's *Werke*, (ed. Walch.), XXI, col. 160 f.
95. *Letters and Papers*, IV, 6627.
96. *Letters and Papers*, IV, 6705.
97. J. Gairdner, *Lollardy and the Reformation*, I, p. 291 f.
98. *Letters and Papers*, IV, 6772.
99. *Letters and Papers*, V, 27.
100. J. Gairdner, *The English Church in the Sixteenth Century*, p. 112.
101. A. F. Pollard, *Henry VIII* (1905), p. 240.
102. J. Gairdner, *op. cit.*, p. 120.
103. *Letters and Papers*, IV, 6111.
104. *Letters and Papers*, V, 361.
105. W. Stubbs, *op. cit.*, p. 294.
106. S. Prüser, *England und die Schmalkaldener* (1929), p. 48 f.
107. Luther, *Briefe* (ed. de Wette), IV, p. 584 f.
108. *loc. cit.*, p. 285 f.
109. S. Prüser, *op. cit.*
110. G. Rupp, *op. cit.*
111. P. Hughes, *op. cit.*, I, 357 f. and II, 23 f.
112. *State Papers, Henry VIII*, vol. VII, 511; 517–18.
113. *Corpus Reformatorum*, II, 1304.
114. Luther's *Briefwechsel* (ed. E. L. Enders), vol. X, 2311.

115. H. de Vocht, *Acta Thomae Mori* (1947).

116. *Corpus Reformatorum*, II, 1381.

117. Friedmann, *op. cit.*, vol. II, p. 84 f.

118. G. Mentz, *Johann Friedrich der Grossmütige* (1903), vol. III, p. 441 f.

119. C. A. H. Burkhardt, *Dr. Martin Luther's Briefwechsel* (1866), p. 233.

120. *Letters and Papers*, IX, 1016.

121. G. Waitz, *Lübeck unter Jürgen Wullenwever und die europäische Politik* (1856), vol. III, p. 221 f.

122. *Letters and Papers*, IX, 153.

123. Luther, *Briefe* (ed. de Wette), vol. IV, p. 662 f.

124. *loc cit.*, p. 668.

125. Mentz, *op. cit.*, vol. III, p. 356.

126. Luther's *Werke* (ed. Walch) vol. XXI, col. 1441.

127. Luther's *Werke* (Erlangen) vol. 55, p. 133 f.

128. *Letters and Papers*, XIII, 352–3.

129. *Letters and Papers*, XIII, 117.

130. *Corpus Reformatorum*, III, 1490.

131. Mont's instructions, *Letters and Papers*, XIII, 367.

132. *Letters and Papers*, XIII, 650.

133. Strype, *op cit.*, I, 2, No. XCIV.

134. Luther, *Briefe* (ed. de Wette), vol. V, p. 110.

135. *Letters and Papers*, XIII, 126.

136. *Letters and Papers*, XIII, 164.

137. Strype, *op. cit.*, I, p. 548.

138. F. A. Cox, *Life of Philip Melanchthon* (1815), p. 412.

139. *Letters and Papers*, XIII, 497.

140. P. Hughes, *op. cit.*, II, p. 12 n.

141. Luther, *Briefe* (ed. de Wette), vol. V, p. 211.

142. *loc. cit.*, p. 213 f.

143. *loc. cit.*, p. 217.

BIBLIOGRAPHY

Allen, P. S., *Opus Epistolarum Des. Erasmi Roterodami*, 7 vols (1906–38).

Anonymus, *Luther und die Bigamie* (Theol. Studien und Kritiken, vol. LXIV, 1891).

Barnes, R., *Bekantnus des Glaubens* (1540).

Bergenroth, G. A. *et al.* (Editors), *Calendar of State Papers, Spanish* (1862 etc.).

Boehmer, H., *Luther and the Reformation in the Light of Modern Research* (1930).

Boree, W., *Heinrich VIII von England und die Curie* (1885).

Brewer, J. S. and Gairdner, J. (Editors), *Calendar of Letters and Papers foreign and domestic, of the Reign of Henry VIII* (1864 etc.).

Bridgett, T. E., *The Life and Writings of Sir Thomas More* (1891).
    The Life of St. John Fisher (4th ed., 1922).
    The Defender of the Faith (1885).

Brown, J. M., *Henry VIII's Book 'Assertio Septem Sacramentorum' and the Royal Title of Defender of the Faith* (Transactions of the Royal Historical Society, vol. VIII, 1880).

Brown, R. (Editor) *Calendar of State Papers . . . relating to English Affairs . . . in the Archives . . . of Venice* (1864 etc.).

Bugenhagen, J., *Von Ehesachen, vom Ehebruch* (1540).
    A compendious letter which Jhon Pomerae . . . sent to the faythfull christen congregation in engelland (1536).

Burnet, G., *The History of the Reformation*, ed. N. Pocock, 7 vols (1865).

Busch, W., *Der Ursprung der Ehescheidung König Heinrichs VIII von England* (Hist. Taschenbuch, 6. Serie, vol. VIII, 1889).

Chambers, R. W., *Thomas More* (1938).

Clemen, O., *Flugschriften aus den ersten Jahren der Reformation*, 4 vols (1907 etc.).
    Beiträge zur Reformationsgeschichte aus Büchern und Handschriften, 3 vols (1900–3).

Clerk, J., *Io. Clerk pro Henrico VIII . . . apud Leonem X . . . in exhibitionis Regii libri . . . oratio* (ca. 1521).

Collier, J., *An Ecclesiastical History of Great Britain*, ed. T. Lathbury, 9 vols (1852).

Constant, G., *The Reformation in England*, 2 vols (1934).

Corpus Reformatorum, ed. Bretschneider *et al.* (1834 etc.).

Cox, F., *Life of Melanchthon* (1815).

Delcourt, J., *Essai sur la Langue de Sir Thomas More* (1914).

Demaus, R., *Tyndale* (1886).

Dickens, A. G., *Lollards and Protestants in the Diocese of York 1509–58* (1959).

Dictionary of National Biography.

Dunkley, E. H., *The Reformation in Denmark* (1948).

Eck, J. von, *Asscritur hic . . . Angliae regis liber de Sacramentis, a calumnis . . . Ludderi* (1532).

Ehse, S., *Römische Dokumente zur Geschichte der Ehescheidung Heinrichs VIII von England* (1893).

Ellis, H., *Original Letters illustrative of English History*, Third Series, vol I (1846).

Emser, H., *Ein sendbrieve Martin Luthers* (1527).
        Bekentnis dass er den Titel auff Luthers sendbrieve . . . gemacht (1527).

Forstemann, C. E., *Neues Urkundenbuch zur Geschichte der evangelischen Kirchenreform* (1842).

Friedmann, P., *Anne Boleyn, a Chapter in English History 1527–36*, 2 vols (1884).

Froude, J. A., *The Divorce of Catherine of Aragon* (1891).

Gairdner, J., *Lollardy and the Reformation*, 4 vols (1908 etc.).
        The English Church in the Sixteenth Century (1902).

Harleian Miscellany, vol. III (1745).

Hauck, A., *Deutschland und England in ihren kirchlichen Beziehungen* (1917).

Henry VIII, *Assertio Septem Sacramentorum* (1521).
        English Translations: by T[homas] W[ebster] (1687).
        (Also a second, revised ed., 1688.)
        In J. Hornihold, *The Commandments and Sacraments explained* (1821).
        (New ed. with an introduction by L. O'Donovan, 1908.)
        In *Henry VIII, Miscellaneous Writings*, ed. F. Macnamara (1924).
        A copy of the letters wherin the most redouted & mighty prince our souerayne lorde kyng Henry the eight . . . made answere unto a certayne letter of Martyn Luther . . . (1536).
        Serenissimi . . . regis Angliae . . . ad . . . Saxoniae principes, de coercenda abingendaque Lutherana factione . . . (1523).

Herbert of Cherbury, Lord, *Life and Reign of Henry VIII* (1682).

Hope, A., *The first Divorce of Henry VIII* (1894).

Hughes, P., *The Reformation in England*, vol. I (1950).

Jacobs, H. E., *The Lutheran Movement in England* (1892).

Kawerau, W., *Thomas Murner und die deutsche Reformation* (1891).

Koestlin, J., *Martin Luther, sein Leben und seine Schriften*, ed. W. Kawerau, 2 vols (1902).

Lepp, F., *Schlagwörter des Reformationszeitalters* (1908).

Lewis, C. S., *English Literature in the Sixteenth Century excluding Drama* (1954).

Lloyd, C., *Formularies of Faith put forth by Authority during the Reign of Henry VIII* (1825).

Loescher, V. E., *Repertorium für die Reformations- and Kirchengeschichte* (1798).

Luther, M., *Sämtliche Werke*, 67 vols, Erlangen (1826–57).

        D. Martin Luthers sowol in Deutscher als latein. Sprache ... sämtliche Schriften, ed. J. G. Walch (1740–50).

        Dr. Martin Luther's Briefwechsel, ed. E. L. Enders, 19 vols (1844–1932).

        Briefe, Sendschreiben und Bedenken ... ed. W. de Wette, 5 vols (1825–28).

        Dr. Martin Luther's Briefwechsel, ed. C. A. H. Burckhardt (1866).

        Contra Henricum Regem Angliae M. Luther (1522).

        Antworth ... M. Luthers auff König Heinrichs von Engelland buch (1522).

        Auff des Königs zu Engelland lesterschrifft titel (1527).

Mattingly, G., *Catherine of Aragon* (1942).

Mentz, G., *Johann Friedrich der Grossmütige*, 3 vols (1903).

        Die Wittenberger Artikel von 1536 (1905).

Meurer, M., *Philip Melanchthons Leben* (1860).

Moeller, W., *Lehrbuch der Kirchengeschichte*, 3 vols (1907).

More, Saint Thomas, (*Rossaus, G.,*) *Eruditissimi viri G. Rossi opus ... quo ... refellit ... Lutheri calumnias ...* (1523).

        Dialogue concerning Tyndale, ed. W. E. Campbell (1927).

Murner, Th., *Ob der künig usz engelland ein lügner sey oder der Luther* (1523).

Myconius, F., *Historia Reformationis* (1718).

Opitz, H., *Heinrich VIII und Sir Thomas More* (1895).

Pauli, R., *Aufsätze zur englischen Geschichte* (1869).

Pocock, N., *Records of the Reformation: The Divorce*, 2 vols (1870).

Pollard, A. F., *Henry VIII* (1905).

        Cranmer (1923).

        Wolsey (1929).

Prüser, S., *England und die Schmalkaldener* (1929).

Reusch, F. H., *Der Index der verboten Bücher* (1883).

Rockwell, W., *Die Doppelehe des Landgrafen Philipp von Hessen* (1904).

Roper, W., *Lyfe of Sir Thomas Moore* (Early English Text Society ed., 1935).

Routh, E. M. G., *Sir Thomas More and his Friends 1477–1535* (1934).

Rupp, E. G., *Studies in the Making of the English Protestant Tradition* (1947).

Schade, O., *Satiren und Pasquillen aus der Reformationszeit*, 3 vols (1856–   ).

Scheible, J., *Das Kloster weltlich und geistlich*, 12 vols (1845–   ).

Siebert, F. S., *Freedom of the Press in England 1476–1776* (1952).

Singer, P., *Beziehungen des Schmalkaldischen Bundes zu England* (1901).

Smith, H. M., *Henry VIII and the Reformation* (1948).

Smith, P., *Henry VIII and Luther* (English Historical Review, vol. XXV).
        German Opinion of the Divorce of Henry VIII (ibid., vol. XXVII).

Smithen, F. J., *Continental Protestantism and the English Reformation* (1927).

State Papers published under the Authority of H.M.'s Commission, *King Henry VIII*, 11 vols (1830 etc.).

Strype, J., *Ecclesiastical Memorials . . . of the Church of England under Henry VIII* (1722).

Sturge, C., *Cuthbert Tunstall* (1938).

Vocht, H. de, *Acta Thomae Mori* (1947).

Waitz, G., *Lübeck unter Jürgen Wullenwever*, 3 vols (1855).

Walther, W., *Henrich der Achte von England und Luther* (1908).

Whitney, J. P., *The History of the Reformation* (2nd ed., 1940).

Wuelcker, E., *Des kursächsischen Rathes Hans v.d. Planitz Berichte . . .* (ed. H. Virck, 1899).

INDEX

Wolsey, Th., Cardinal, 4, 5, 7, 8, 10,
12, 14, 15, 16, 19, 20, 22, 39, 50,
53, 55, 59, 65, 67, 68, 69, 84,
102, 126

Worms, Diet of, 4, 5, 8
Wullenwever, J., 100

Zwingli, H., 12, 85, 110